THE LANCASHIRE FIGHTING TERRITORIALS

"HOW CAN A COMMANDER SAY ENOUGH FOR THE TROOPS WHO, AWARE THAT THEIR TASK WAS ONLY A SUBSIDIARY ONE, FOUGHT WITH JUST AS MUCH VIM AND RESOLUTION AS IF THEY WERE STORMING THE BATTLEMENTS OF CONSTANTINOPLE?" (*Sir Ian Hamilton on the East Lancashires, in his dispatch, December* 11, 1915).

THE
LANCASHIRE FIGHTING TERRITORIALS

BY
GEORGE BIGWOOD

The Naval & Military Press Ltd

Published by

The Naval & Military Press Ltd
Unit 5 Riverside, Brambleside
Bellbrook Industrial Estate
Uckfield, East Sussex
TN22 1QQ England

Tel: +44 (0)1825 749494

www.naval-military-press.com
www.nmarchive.com

Cover Illustration:
A boat carrying Lancashire Fusiliers, bound for Gallipoli. Photo by Ernest Brooks. When the Gallipoli landings were being prepared, Winston Churchill arranged for there to be journalists and photographers accompanying the expeditionary force. Brooks, as a professional photographer already in uniform, was appointed as the Admiralty official photographer.

In reprinting in facsimile from the original, any imperfections are inevitably reproduced and the quality may fall short of modern type and cartographic standards.

FOREWORD

By GENERAL SIR IAN S. M. HAMILTON,
G.C.B., D.S.O., A.D.C. General to the King, late General Officer Commanding-in-Chief Mediterranean Expeditionary Force

" To write a brief Foreword to a work wherein the war services of the Lancashire Territorials may, it is hoped, be imperishably recorded."

Such a request is an honour to the recipient ; to comply with it is much more than an honour : it is a real pleasure, and yet, in some sense, also an embarrassment.

Already my dispatches have borne witness, as best they might, to the valour of the Lancastrians. Were I to relabour that old ground, surely the bread would be taken out of the mouth of the author.

Here, then, is something, inadequate certainly, but fresh ; an extract from my private diary exhibiting these young heroes impartially—exhibiting them before they had left the Egyptian command or had yet an idea that they were to dazzle imagination by their exploit.

"*Cairo, March* 28.—Inspected East Lancashire Division and a Yeomanry Brigade (Westminster Dragoons and Herts). How I envied Maxwell these lovely lads ! No chance to use them here with summer coming up and the desert getting as dry as a bone. What wouldn't I give to carry them off with me *now*. These Lancashire men especially are eye-openers. How on earth have they managed to pick up the swank and devil-may-care airs of crack Regulars? They *are* Regulars, only they are bigger, more effective specimens than Manchester mills or East Lancashire mines can spare us for the regular service in peace time. Anyway, no soldier need wish to see a finer lot. On them has descended the mantle of my old comrades of Elandslaagte and Caesar's Camp, and worthily beyond doubt they will wear it."

The enthusiasm of the natives was a pleasing part of the show. During four years of Egyptian inspections I can recall no instances of any manifestations of friendliness to our troops, or even of interest in them by Gyppies. But the Territorials seem, somehow, to have conquered their goodwill. As each stalwart company swung past there was a spontaneous effervescence of waving hands along the crowded street and murmurs of applause from Bedouin, Blacks, and Fellaheen.

IAN HAMILTON.

POSTLIP HALL,
May 31, 1916.

CONTENTS

	PAGES
FOREWORD BY GENERAL SIR IAN S. M. HAMILTON, G.C.B., D.S.O.	v
INTRODUCTION BY THE AUTHOR	1
BATTLE OF THE SUEZ CANAL	17, 137, 151
ROYAL ENGINEERS (FIELD AND SIGNAL COMPANIES)	28, 137, 151

LANCASHIRE FUSILIERS BRIGADE:

5TH BATTALION LANCASHIRE FUSILIERS (BURY)	34, 138, 151
6TH BATTALION LANCASHIRE FUSILIERS (ROCHDALE)	42, 139, 152
7TH BATTALION LANCASHIRE FUSILIERS (SALFORD)	52, 140, 152
8TH BATTALION LANCASHIRE FUSILIERS (SALFORD)	62, 141, 152

MANCHESTER INFANTRY BRIGADE:

5TH BATTALION MANCHESTER REGIMENT (WIGAN)	72, 142, 152
6TH BATTALION MANCHESTER REGIMENT	77, 143, 152
7TH BATTALION MANCHESTER REGIMENT	87, 145, 153
8TH BATTALION MANCHESTER REGIMENT	102, 146, 153

Contents

EAST LANCASHIRE BRIGADE :

    4TH BATTALION EAST LANCASHIRE REGIMENT (BLACKBURN) 109, 149, 153

    5TH BATTALION EAST LANCASHIRE REGIMENT (BURNLEY) 112, 149, 154

    9TH BATTALION MANCHESTER REGIMENT (ASHTON) 117, 147, 154

    10TH BATTALION MANCHESTER REGIMENT (OLDHAM) 121, 148, 154

FIELD AMBULANCES (ROYAL ARMY MEDICAL CORPS) 124, 150, 154

GREAT BUT UNAVAILING GALLANTRY : WHY ? . 132

HONOURS AND REWARDS. 136

ROLL OF HONOUR 151

APPENDIX—THE OPERATIONS IN EGYPT . . . 155

EAST LANCASHIRE'S FIGHTING TERRITORIALS

INTRODUCTION

"When Can Their Glory Fade?"

" In sooth, if valour's noblest part be this,
  Nobly to die
By fate's award, we shall not miss,
  For here we lie.
Striving to crown our land with Freedom's bays,
  Death we disdained ;
And time shall never mar the meed of praise
  That valour gained.

" The land they loved shall wear the fadeless crown
    Her warriors gave her
When, wrapped in death's dark cloud, they laid them down,
    Dying to save her.
Yet, being dead, they die not ; in the grave
    Tho' they be lying,
These be the souls to whom high valour gave
    Glory undying." *

By the waters of the Aegean many gallant East Lancashire Territorials have made the supreme sacrifice. Amid war's lightning flashes they nobly redeemed the promise they made when they left Lancashire : To make a reputation for the Division. Their motto was : " For King and

---

* Lines written by Simonides of Cos in honour of those who fell with Leonidas. From Mr. Pott's *Translations of Greek Love Songs and Epigrams* (Kegan Paul, Trench, Trübner & Co.).

country." From it they gathered their inspiration, and by their deeds and unquestioning obedience to duty they proved to their admiring countrymen how highly they valued it. On that Peninsula of desolation where our troops showed unexampled gallantry—they never fought but to conquer—there is still some hallowed ground. " They died for their King and country," is the brief but all-sufficient message left by their comrades on the cliff immediately above " Lancashire Landing." The cemetery there came to be known as " Lancashire Heroes Corner."

How did our Territorials face the ordeal of battle? They marched into the bullet-swept area as though it were just an event of little more than ordinary importance. Their nonchalance suggested that they did not fully appreciate the fact that at last they were to be put to the severe test of actually doing in war what they had so often simulated in peace. Had the phrase " the grim realities of war" any serious meaning for them? They certainly had the appearance of being quite cool and collected; they looked a determined set of men, and one could not doubt their courage. The purpose of this book is to pass in review some of the achievements by which they have earned renown.

The psychology of the soldier as he marches for the first time, tired and heavy-laden, into the fire-swept zone is an interesting study. The patriotic emotions are not now stirred by the martial roll of drums; the signal to " charge " is not sounded on the bugle; standards are not there to encourage and foster the fighting spirit. Yet, in the absence of these concomitants of war, in the absence of all the " pomp and circumstance " of earlier fighting which influenced so greatly the combatants on either side, our men, in this dull, this gruesome, largely mechanical, subterranean campaign, have brought disillusionment to those who regarded the British soldier as a mere automaton in the absence of the military "aids" of drums and flags. Our soldiers—our Territorials—have shown initiative of a very high order, and they have attempted the most daring and dangerous operations; often with astonishing success. It is not possible, in any written account, adequately to measure the heroism and fortitude which have been so conspicuously displayed. General Sir Ian Hamilton has comprehended all in the one word—"magnificent."

Any description of a modern battle which professes to record individual instances of heroism must be conspicuous not for what it records, but for what it leaves unrecorded. In the stress and struggle of continuous fighting at Gallipoli neither officer nor man is able to do more than describe what actually happened to himself or to his comrade at his side; and when a battalion enters a fight 1,000 strong, and is reduced to 500 before nightfall, it is safe to say that many officers and men among the fallen have shown conspicuous bravery who are merely recorded among the killed or wounded in the casualty list. General (now Sir) William Douglas wrote of the 7th Manchesters (Colonel Gresham's Battalion), that the cause of the relatively small number of the gallant deeds recorded during the Gallipoli operations was the lack of witnesses due to the heavy casualties. But we have it on the authority of Sir Ian Hamilton that the East Lancashires exhibited marvellous courage and endurance, a cheerful and serene heroism, a contempt for danger; a consuming desire to overcome the enemy and to add lustre to British arms.

This war has taught us many things, and among them this—that our Territorials are not the fair-weather soldiers that many of their detractors in pre-war days had declared them to be. We have yet to learn what a great debt we owe to our Territorials. Organised and equipped on the regular army basis (and to Lord Haldane's practical grasp of the requirements of our Territorial organisation during the time he was at the War Office we are indebted for this), the Territorial Army (of all arms) reinforced our small but highly trained and redoubtable professional army at a grave crisis in our national history, and from all quarters have come reports telling of their courage, their devotion to duty, and their endurance in some of the stiffest fighting recorded in history.

The East Lancashire Divisional units were mobilised early in August 1914, and approximately 90 per cent. of the men volunteered for Imperial Service. After two weeks' "standing to arms" at their respective headquarters, the troops were moved to training camps near Bolton, Bury, and Rochdale; and in the latter end of September, Major-General Sir William Douglas, C.B., K.C.M.G., D.S.O., General Officer Commanding, received secret orders to proceed with his Division to Egypt. Officers and men were anxious to get into the fighting area, and when it leaked out that they might be " shipped somewhere east of Suez " instead of proceeding direct to Flanders (the Gallipoli Peninsula was not at this time considered as a possible fighting area), great disappointment was expressed. Several of the officers (since killed) told me on the eve of their departure that they were anxious to see some fighting ; that they wanted to do something more than garrison duty. They had trained with regular soldiers in peace, and they now wished to co-operate with them in war. But the order was to "move to Egypt," and it was not theirs to reason why. About forty special trains transferred the men, horses, guns, and other war *matériel* to Southampton, where the whole Division (less one Brigade of Artillery) embarked for their great adventure. The troops were in the highest spirits as they crowded on to the transports; they were ready to go anywhere and to do anything. For six months the East Lancashires were on service in Egypt. Some were at Cairo ; others at Alexandria. They spent their time up to Christmas 1914 digging trenches in the

Introduction

most approved manner, marching, skirmishing, and generally simulating war. At a later date the engagement with the Turks on the Suez Canal by the Blackburn and Bolton Artillery and the Royal Engineers, and the occupation of Cyprus by a detachment of the 8th Manchesters, brought the Lancashires to a closer realisation of the value of the services they were rendering their King and country.

In December (1914) General Douglas sent me a private letter (which I am now at liberty to make public) in which he described the progress made in the training of the troops, and alluded to their soldierly conduct and their desire to march against the enemy. General Douglas wrote:

> "I got all the troops together and marched through Cairo. I have asked Colonel Tufnell [General Douglas's staff officer, now Brigadier General commanding the East Lancashire Infantry Brigade] to send you a copy of the letter Sir John Maxwell wrote to me afterwards, and I now enclose a cutting from the *Egyptian Mail*. Unfortunately I could not get all the units on parade. The Manchester Brigade was unrepresented, the Field Companies Royal Engineers, and a large portion of the Signal Company are on the Suez Canal, and we have many guards and duties to find, but the column was over four miles long, and the parade was greater than anything seen in Cairo before. The men marched splendidly, the streets, or rather pavements (for the streets were kept by the police clear of traffic) were packed with people, who expressed their approval by clapping their hands and shouting, 'Vive les Anglais!' It was quite impressive, and I fancy it must have opened the eyes of many. The men are working well and behaving splendidly."

The following is an extract from Divisional Orders issued by General Douglas in connection with this parade: "It is with great satisfaction that the Major-General places on record the following letter which he has received from Headquarters. He congratulates the troops on their hard and willing work, which has earned for them this recognition of their increasing efficiency":

Introduction

"Lieutenant-General Sir John Maxwell, commanding the forces in Egypt, desires to express to you his admiration of the turn-out and marching of the division at this morning's parade. It was in all respects excellent; the men looked fit and hard. The improvement in the short time they have been in Egypt is quite remarkable. All arms—artillery, cavalry, and infantry, as well as the Royal Army Medical Corps—showed that they had been working hard, with good results, and the Lieutenant-General will have great pleasure in reporting to the Secretary of State for War the improvement in general efficiency of all ranks of the Territorial Force in Egypt, and he is quite sure that no effort will be spared to attain that efficiency, brought about by attention to detail and discipline, which will enable them to take their place in the first line of His Majesty's Army."

The *Egyptian Mail* made the following comment on the parade:

"Cairo yesterday had its first opportunity of giving a welcome to the Territorial regiments recently arrived in this country, and a hearty one it was. The crowds along the line of march were much more enthusiastic than is their usual wont on such occasions, and the cheering in the Sharia Kamel, where the crowd was perhaps as dense as anywhere, testified plainly to the admiration evoked by the soldierly bearing and fine marching of the troops. There was no question but that here was fighting material of the best quality, of which any nation might well be proud. The Germans in high places have been considerably disillusioned already—they would have been still more disillusioned, both as to the attitude of the Egyptian people and as to the calibre of our Territorials, had any of them been in the streets of Cairo yesterday."

In a later communication General Douglas wrote:

"I am sorry to say that Lieutenant Wood and six non-commissioned officers and men of one of the Field Companies R.E. were drowned in the Suez Canal on December 17. The boiler of a steam launch they were on exploded. Their sad death is deplored by everyone. They were working at the Canal defences at the time. Both the Field Companies have done most excellent work there, and have won the praise of Sir John Maxwell and all those under whose observation they have come.

"Everyone has been working splendidly, and the way in which the men have carried out long days of tactical exercises on the

Introduction

sand desert is beyond praise and speaks well for their spirit and physique. They are bronzed soldiers now, and their friends at home would be astonished to see how they have developed in so short a time."

The threatened invasion of Egypt by the Turks developed early in February, and among the troops detailed to offer resistance were batteries of the Bolton and Blackburn Brigades of Field Artillery, and the Field Companies Royal Engineers. The main attack on the Canal was delivered at Tussum, near Ismailia, on February 3, and minor attacks were simultaneously made on other parts of the Canal. It is computed that 12,000 Turks took part in the operations. Our troops were well entrenched and ready to deliver their attack at what was considered to be the most opportune time. This was when some progress had been made in the construction of a pontoon bridge on the Canal. The Turks were "surprised" shortly after daybreak, and the engagement continued for about eight hours. The Turks by this time had fled, leaving a large number of their killed and wounded on the field. In a description of the battle a correspondent referred in the following terms to the Lancashire Territorials' share of the fighting:

"They were not numerously represented, but a very important though comparatively small portion of the Territorials was on the Canal, and I have it on the best authority that during a very hot period of the fight they behaved with admirable coolness and self-possession. At one time they were under a heavy shell-fire, and were ordered to shelter in the trenches, but they maintained a perfect discipline and calmness worthy of the traditions of the regiments of which they are the Territorial units."

One of the pontoons—it is made of galvanised iron—is now in the possession of the Manchester Corporation as a war relic. It was sent to the city by General Douglas.

On March 28 General Sir Ian Hamilton, commanding the Mediterranean Expeditionary Force, reviewed the

East Lancashire Division at Cairo. The following order was subsequently issued:

" General Sir Ian Hamilton, having been accorded the privilege of reviewing the East Lancashire Division, wishes to congratulate the General Officer Commanding the troops in Egypt, as well as Major-General Douglas, on the turn-out and soldierly bearing of that force.

" He was able to observe to-day that the East Lancashire Division has made full use of the advantages which continuous fine weather and the absence of billeting have given them over their comrades now bearing arms, whether at home or on the Continent of Europe.

" Ever since the siege of Ladysmith, General Sir Ian Hamilton has interested himself specially in the military output of Manchester, and it is a real pleasure to him now to be able to bear witness to the fact that this great city is being so finely represented in the East."

Major-General W. Douglas, in issuing the order, said that all ranks would welcome the signal recognition of the discipline, efficiency, and sterling good qualities of the Division. Lieutenant-General Sir John Maxwell, commanding the forces in Egypt, said he specially asked Sir Ian Hamilton to review the Division because of his unique experience at home. It was, therefore, with pride that he could report that Sir Ian endorsed the opinion he (Sir John) had forwarded to the Secretary for War.

A month after this review (the first week in May), the East Lancashires were crossing to the Dardanelles, where they have won imperishable fame. Dare we count the cost! The troops in Gallipoli set out to win a victory which promised to turn to our favour the whole course of the war. Had they accomplished their aim, the sacrifice, great as it has been, would have been borne with resignation, if not with composure. Having failed in that field to achieve success, we are naturally inclined to dwell on the statistical side—to measure the loss of so many brave fellows against the gains obtained in behalf

Introduction

of the allied cause. But we have this assurance: that where our troops failed no other troops could have succeeded.

June 4, 1915, will ever be a memorable day in the history of the East Lancashire Territorials. When "Gallipoli, 1915," has been inscribed on the colours carried by the infantry battalions we shall salute them with greater solemnity than ever before. Recalling the glorious Fourth of June, and the officers and men who fell on that and subsequent days during a brilliant assault on the Turkish position, we shall involuntarily pay our respects to the memory of those who, whilst placing different values on life, readily, uncomplainingly, indeed cheerfully, went to their death in a glorious endeavour to uphold the best traditions of an anti-militaristic and freedom-loving country. General Sir William Douglas sent me the following message in which he pays a great tribute to his troops:

"The division has done exceedingly well. The Manchester Brigade and the Lancashire Fusiliers Brigade of the infantry have seen most of the fighting, and have shown a fine spirit, and nobly upheld the honour of the Territorial Force. The Manchester Brigade, together with one battalion of the Lancashire Fusiliers, carried out the brilliant assault of June 4, which won the admiration of Sir Ian Hamilton and of the whole force. It was the centre which got forward and carried three lines of trenches, but owing to those on the right and left not being able to push through we were obliged to give up some of the most forward trenches. But the men held on to the foremost line until I ordered them back, and I did not do that until I saw that they would have been cut off owing to their flanks being uncovered.

"This tenacity on their part was the best feature of the action. It is a small matter to carry trenches compared to the holding of them under such circumstances. I am told that the language of the men, on finding that they had to withdraw from the foremost trench won, was perfectly appalling. I like that, for it shows the right spirit.

"Our artillery, or rather the portion of it that is here, has done magnificently. It has called forth the highest praise, and I hope that it may meet with the reward which it richly deserves.

The gunners have shown a devotion to duty, a disregard of danger, and an endurance which are worthy of the best traditions of the British Army.

"The Convalescent Home at Alexandria, which is being managed by Mrs. (now Lady) Douglas, and which is being supported by the generous gifts of the people of East Lancashire, is a very great success. It is spoken of as the model home. It has been inspected by the principal officers of the medical services and the Red Cross Society, all of whom have spoken of it in the highest terms. The men themselves who have been patients there speak of it as ' Paradise.' "

In another communication to Colonel R. Cecil Winder, Secretary to the East Lancashire Territorial Association, General Douglas said:

" In the big attack on June 4, the Manchester Brigade and half the 5th Fusiliers were in the first line. I can only produce Sir Ian Hamilton's words and say ' it was brilliantly done.' Nothing could have exceeded the dash of the men.

" The action was commenced at 8 a.m., by a heavy bombardment of the Turkish trenches with shrapnel and gun-fire. This was going on until just before 12 noon, when shrapnel alone was fired at an increased range.

" Punctually at twelve o'clock the men dashed forward, and jumped the Turks' wire entanglements and posts which had been broken by high-explosive shells, and went straight into the trenches. At 12.10 these were in our hands. Then the second line went forward, jumped over the Turks' first line and advanced quickly on to the second line. This they reached and captured by 12.32 p.m. Not content with this, they continued their advance and lost men. Alas! the division on our right and left had been unable to advance as well. Thus our men had both flanks exposed. In spite of that they held on for some hours.

" On the left were the 5th Manchesters (Wigan), and though their flank was turned and the Turks were almost in the rear, they did not give way until ordered to do so. Then they fell back on to the Turkish first line, which was in our hands and which we have still got a very tight hold of.

" On June 6 the Turks made a heavy counter-attack. They came on in masses and could not make progress. We held our line (until lately theirs) firmly. Young —— was splendid. With a machine gun on our left he literally mowed down the Turkish

Introduction

masses until he had built up a high parapet of their bodies. That counter-attack was begun at 3 a.m. and died away in the evening.

"Our fellows were simply splendid. Nothing I can say will convey to you the magnificent fighting spirit they showed.

"The Turks behave like gentlemen to our wounded, as they have done all through. Some of our wounded we recovered were skilfully bandaged, and they said that officers had given them cigarettes, shaken hands with them, and congratulated them on the splendid attack they had made.

"People in Lancashire may well be proud of their fellow-citizens. Brigadier-General Noel Lee (late commander of the Manchester Infantry Brigade), as you may imagine, is a very great loss to the Division."

Sir Ian Hamilton, after this big attack, cabled to the Lord Mayor of Manchester and the Mayor of Salford, from Tenedos:

"I think you will appreciate a message direct from the front to tell you how admirably your citizen soldiers bore themselves in the battle of the 4th and 5th of June, when, together with the other East Lancastrians, they carried three lines of entangled trenches at the point of the bayonet. All serving here admire their conduct and regret their losses."

In the thrilling dispatch from Sir Ian Hamilton published in September (1914) further praise is given to the Lancashire Territorials. The advance of the Manchesters on June 4 the General describes as "magnificent," and as regards the Royal Engineers, the Signal Service, the Army Service Corps, and the Royal Army Medical Corps, General Hamilton paid a tribute to their efficiency and heroism in their difficult and dangerous tasks.

"The question was now," writes the Commander-in-Chief, "whether this rolling up of the newly captured line from the right would continue until the whole of our gains were wiped out. It looked very like it, for now the enfilade fire of the Turks began to fall upon the Manchester Brigade of the 42nd Division, which was firmly consolidating the farthest distant line of trenches it had so brilliantly won. After 1.30 p.m. it became increasingly difficult for this gallant Brigade to hold its ground. Heavy casualties occurred; the Brigadier and many other officers were wounded or killed. Yet it continued to hold out with the greatest tenacity and grit. Every effort was made to sustain the Brigade in its position. Its right flank was thrown back to make face against the enfilade fire, and reinforcements were sent to try to fill the diagonal gap between it and the Royal Naval Division. But ere long it became clear that unless the right of our line could advance again, it would be impossible for the Manchesters to maintain the very pronounced salient in which they now found themselves. Orders were issued, therefore, that the Royal Naval Division should co-operate with the French corps in a fresh attack, and reinforcements were dispatched to this end. The attack timed for 3 p.m. was twice postponed at the request of General Gouraud, who finally reported that he would be unable to advance again that day with any prospect of success. By 6.30 p.m., therefore, the 42nd (East Lancashire Territorial) Division had to be extricated with loss from the second-line trenches, and had to content themselves with consolidating on the first line, which they had captured within five minutes of commencing the attack. Such was the spirit displayed by this (Manchester) Brigade, that there was great difficulty in persuading the men to fall back. Had their flanks been covered, nothing would have made them loosen their grip."

Sir Ian Hamilton adds that although they had been forced to abandon so much of the ground gained in the first rush, the net result of the day's operations was considerable—namely, an advance of 200 to 400 yards along the whole of their centre, a front of nearly three miles. The enemy suffered severely. The prisoners taken during the day amounted to 400, including 11 officers; amongst these were 5 Germans, the remains of a volunteer machine-gun detachment from the *Goeben*. Their commanding officer was killed and the machine gun destroyed. The majority of these captures were made by the 42nd (East Lancashire) Division, under Major-General Sir William Douglas.

On October 17, 1915, General Douglas, in behalf of his troops, sent the following message to the General Officer Commanding:

" Forty-second Division wish to express their deep regret on hearing of your departure. We all thank you for your invariable kindness and consideration, and wish you God-speed,"

Introduction

Sir Ian Hamilton sent the following reply to the General Officer Commanding the 42nd Division :

" Please tell the 42nd Division that their sympathetic message reached me by wireless, and put fresh heart into me on my voyage home. I have now had the double privilege of commanding the Manchesters throughout the siege of Ladysmith and the 42nd Division during their five months' ceaseless struggle on the Gallipoli Peninsula, and, knowing them thus, I say there is no one can beat the East Lancashire lads for loyalty and grit."

Last Christmas Day the General Officer Commanding the 42nd Division kindly sent me a further message in which he related one or two individual acts of bravery :

"The Division," he writes, "is still doing splendidly. The 6th and 7th Lancashire Fusiliers did very good work from the 19th to the 21st inst. They captured a Turkish trench, and were driven out by a counter-attack, but in a quarter of an hour they got it back and we still hold it. Major Law was unfortunately killed. His loss is very great. Through the campaign he has shown the greatest gallantry, initiative, and determination. The men were devoted to him and would follow him anywhere.

" The 7th and 8th Manchesters did equally good work a few days ago, and the 9th Manchesters also.

" Some very daring reconnaissances have been made. A lance-corporal crawled over our parapet to a crater about forty yards away and close to the trench of the Turks. The enemy had a sap which led through a tunnel under their parapet to the crater. The man got into the sap, walked along it and through the tunnel, crept for 20 yards up to the Turkish trench, then back and 20 yards below the tunnel, took the dimensions of the work, and returned safely with the information. This was done at night.

" Here is another instance of heroic conduct. An officer crept up to a Turkish trench last week, looked over the parapet and spotted the entrance to one of their mine shafts by the glow of a light that was coming from it. The next night he called for three volunteers to destroy this shaft entrance. The arrangements were to carry out 40 pounds of gelignite, some electric wire, and a thin rope. The entrance to the sap was blinded with railway sleepers. Mottershead carried the gelignite (which was slung round his neck) and the rope. He crawled out, followed by Downton, who carried the wire. When they came to the

Turks' entanglements they happily found a gap through which they crawled—all this time the electric wire was being laid—and when Mottershead reached the spot where the blindage ended he placed his charge on the edge of it, having previously fixed the electric wire to the charge and to the rope. Now his troubles were to begin. It was necessary to lay the rope straight and diagonally across the ground between the point at which the charge was laid and our position. The idea was to pull the rope slightly so that the gelignite would fall off the blindage into the mouth of the shaft. To do this he had to get over the wire entanglements—(no easy job by day)—at night with Turks within a few feet of him. This is heroism. He surmounted the entanglement difficulty successfully, and reached our trench with the end of the rope. A slight pull of the rope was given which released the electric current, the mine shaft was demolished and the Turkish miners were buried. This mine led under one of our posts and in a few hours it would have been blown up. This gallant action saved us."

The first chapter of war service of the East Lancashire Territorials contains many stirring incidents of this character. It ended with the evacuation of Gallipoli with the dawn of 1916. They landed on the Peninsula early in May 1915, marched straight into the fight, and for three months they were in the firing line and reserve without relief. During this time the Lancashires took part in three big attacks, and were subjected to the continuous strain of holding, improving, and extending the lines of communications under constant fire. During this arduous period the men " displayed a dash in attack and a spirit of determination and endurance in defence which is worthy of the best traditions of the British Army."

" None linger now upon the plain
Save those who ne'er shall fight again."

The East Lancashire Division left the Peninsula with but a remnant of its former self. It bore the appearance of an army that had struggled gallantly against overwhelming odds. It was a war-stained, a sadly depleted, but not in any sense a broken army. A measure of cheerfulness pervaded the ranks as " all that were left of them " returned to " Lancashire Landing," where their comrades of the Line had won imperishable glory. But it was a cheerfulness of the heroic type, for there was much to make them sad. They were leaving behind so many of their comrades who were honoured, beloved, and mourned.

" For some time," writes an officer, " we listened to the sea breaking at our feet, and watched the stars sink into the sea in the west. Then someone started singing ' By yon bonnie banks and yon bonnie braes,' and the lads from Rochdale, Todmorden, and Middleton by the shore of the Aegean sea sang with a pathos and depth of meaning that will never be forgotten. Then ' Annie Laurie ' was started, and was followed by ' O come, all ye faithful,' ' All people that on earth do dwell,' and others, old and new, learned in far-off Sunday school or nearer barrack-room."

Major-General Sir William Douglas, during the stress of military duties after the evacuation, kindly sent me the following message in which he refers in terms of the highest admiration to the great soldierly qualities displayed by his troops in a particularly arduous, and from many points of view quite exceptional, campaign :

" I am filled with admiration at the fine fighting qualities and endurance shown by the men of the Division. Given good leaders, nothing will stop them. No soldiers have been put to a greater test than those in the Gallipoli Peninsula campaign.
" From the beginning of May up to the very end of December these Lancashire lads, many of them mere boys, were in the fighting line. Throughout the heat of summer—the flies a veritable plague—with much dysentery and other troubles, these youngsters dug and fought day and night, and yet were always in good spirits. I am proud indeed to command such gallant fellows."

In the following pages I have attempted to supply a record, which must necessarily be brief, of the work in the field of each unit of the 42nd (East Lancashire) Division. The record, in no instance, makes any pretence to be complete. For obvious reasons it is impossible, at this early period, adequately to give in detail all the achievements of our brave men in Gallipoli. The most that can be done is to show how their loyalty and devotion to duty inspired them to great deeds; how that with a singleness of aim and fervour in execution they added to the glory of British arms and won the highest praise from that distinguished General, Sir Ian Hamilton, and from their Divisional Commander, Major-General Sir William Douglas.

The East Lancashire Territorials have been raised from the depths of scorn and neglect to the highest pinnacle of fame.

GEORGE BIGWOOD.

30, WHITELOW ROAD,
    CHORLTON-CUM-HARDY,
        MANCHESTER.

Easter, 1916.

BATTLE OF SUEZ CANAL

Lancashire Gunners Fight in the Desert

A BATTERY of four guns lies hidden in gun pits on the bank of the Suez Canal. Each gun (of 15-pr. calibre) peeped threateningly over the miles of sandy desert which lay before it, silently waiting for the movement of a hostile force. In the rear of the guns the horses were tethered, and in a line of tents under cover of the canal bank lived about 150 men who were daily expecting their first call to man the guns and to throw shrapnel against an enemy. From an observation station on the canal bank an officer, with the aid of powerful field glasses, searched the desert near and far for any sinister movement of armed troops. Days passed, weeks passed—and all the time the same strict vigilance was kept over this part of the canal bank. The officer saw nothing to create any alarm; patrols which quietly and secretly reconnoitred the front had not observed anything calculated to rouse their suspicions. There was no sign of armed hostilities. Calm reigned everywhere. But it was the calm that preludes a storm. Meanwhile the men in the rear were watching and waiting, drilling, digging gun emplacements, and performing other exercises. They were just keeping themselves fit for the strenuous life to come.

This was a Lancashire Territorial Battery. In the Army List it is officially designated the 5th Lancashire Battery of the 1st East Lancashire Brigade, Royal Field Artillery, with headquarters at Church, near Accrington.

Perhaps we were a little apprehensive about the gunners' share in this great adventure. They were not professional gunners; they were not accustomed to horses. From their youth up they had toiled in the cotton mills and weaving sheds of Lancashire, spinning yarn and weaving cloth. Their experience of this scientific branch of British arms was gained in a fleeting camp. They drilled and manœuvred for a fortnight in each year, provided there was sufficient ground at their disposal (and it often happened that there was not), and paraded the streets contiguous to their headquarters in Lancashire. As for gun practice, they were accorded the privilege of firing live shell when a range was available. What could these men know of the science of gunnery? The professional gunner despised them; the public, without knowledge of their potential value as soldiers, derided them. But a cataclysmic change altered our perspective, and all who professed and called themselves soldiers were acclaimed for their patriotism and self-sacrifice.

The stranger in Egypt, who had not the privilege of previous acquaintance with these men, consoled himself with the thought that the Lancashires came of a good " fighting stock " and that the " material " was " promising," that it bore the unmistakable impress of daring and determination. One who has been in close contact with them for the past fifteen years, both at home and in training camps, and who knew them to be imperfectly trained (through no fault either of the officers or men) in consequence of the difficulties that impeded their development in every direction, held most optimistic opinions about their self-sacrifice, their devotion, their courage, and their patriotism. My firm conviction was that after a period of continuous efficient training they would be fine men to have in a tight corner—that they would dare to do anything, like their comrades of the professional army.

Surprise for Turks

In time of peace they had asked to be taken seriously. The response to that appeal reached them in Egypt. This was their first experience of active service, and the cool and collected manner in which they performed their allotted tasks when shelled by the Turks, the complete self-possession they showed when serving the guns, and their remarkably effective fire removed all signs of uneasiness that had been apparent when it was suggested that the Lancashire Territorial gunners should supply the guns and assist to repel the impending invasion.

The Turks hoped to effect a surprise. They were permitted to approach the Canal under cover of darkness, and at some points to begin their pontoon building. But it was our troops who created a surprise for the Turks. Their progress across the camel tracks had been watched, their strength noted, their dispositions recorded, their direction followed, and their rate of marching measured. We knew approximately what time they would reach the Canal and what would be their approximate strength at various points. Patrols had been withdrawn in order to delude them, and the troops of the Indian Expeditionary Force, the New Zealanders, and the Lancashire Territorial Artillery lay securely entrenched and for the time inert. The Turks began their bridging operations, and in the absence of any sign of opposition they felt secure. Suddenly, at a given signal, machine gun and rifle fire wrought terrible confusion among the ranks of Turkey. They had been caught in a trap. The bridging operations were wrecked, prisoners were taken, others were shot down, and one strong detachment had their retirement seriously checked. The enemy was completely overwhelmed and crushed. In this sharp and short conflict the Lancashire gunners behaved splendidly. Our list of casualties included some brave Bolton men.

Brigadier-General A. D'A. King, D.S.O., who commands the East Lancashire Divisional Artillery, assisted by his Brigade-Major, Major L. W. La T. Cockcraft, had issued orders allocating certain positions along the Canal bank to each of the three batteries of the Blackburn and of the Bolton Brigades. The Church Battery, commanded by Major J. C. Browning, took up an entrenched position near Port Said. The screen of skirmishers occupying the bank in front of the guns was supplied by a New Zealand contingent, and a detachment of native cavalry patrolled that part of the desert from which the attack was expected to come. One day in January the desert was completely blotted out by a terrific sandstorm. Nothing could be seen; the troops were completely at the mercy of this tornadic visitation. But the reports of patrols on the previous day and also of the observing officers gave promise of an early attack.

In the early hours of the following morning the troops heard the rattle of musketry. They were under fire. Bullets were flying in every direction. It was now clear that the Turks had taken advantage of the storm of the previous day to advance upon the Canal. But the attempt to invade Egypt was foredoomed to failure. The troops of the Indian Expeditionary Force, some Indian Lancers, a camel corps, and some guns were there to meet the invaders. The Lancashire Battery was on the tiptoe of expectation. Major Browning gave instructions that no man was to leave his tent. Later the men were paraded in front of their camp, and Major Browning reported that it was impossible for the gunners to do anything in the darkness, but they must hold themselves in readiness.

The Canal at this point is about 100 yards wide, and along the embankment there are big entrenchments. The Turks got up to the bank and opened fire, to which the New Zealanders replied. Before the return of daylight the invading army beat a hasty retreat. Little is

Shelling the Enemy

known of the strength of the force that effected this surprise. But their sudden appearance and equally sudden disappearance suggest that it was a small raiding party sent out to test the strength of the army of occupation.

The General Officer Commanding decided at once to take the offensive. At night the Lancashire gunners received orders hurriedly to prepare to cross the Canal and harass the enemy, for it had been reported by the flying scouts that he was in strong force some miles across the desert and looked likely to attack. A pontoon bridge was thrown across the waterway, and the infantry, cavalry, a camel corps, and the Church Battery left at 6 a.m. to punish the enemy for his escapade on the previous night and to destroy any plans he may have evolved for further trespass. A detachment of New Zealanders was " told off " to act as an escort for the guns, and some cavalry provided a protecting screen. The infantry advanced across the desert in skirmishing order, and in the folds of sand they were soon out of sight. The gunners moved off later when the cavalry escort reported a clear road. Some miles away from the Canal bank the guns took up a position under cover of the sand dunes, and a target in the form of a mass of Turks offered just the opportunity that Major Browning and his men had been waiting for. The unlimbering was smartly done, the drivers galloped their horses to cover, the gunners trained their guns on to the spot indicated by the range officer, the fuse was set, and away went the first shell (if the range finding has been good and the fuse setting satisfactory, which is hardly likely at this early stage of the fight) to throw a spray of bullets among the enemy. The first range at which the shells were fired was 3,000 yards. Then the fuses were lengthened to catch the retiring army. Altogether above fifty rounds were fired, but at no time did the Turks reply. They were evidently not prepared to engage long-range gun fire.

The Turks were driven back with loss. On our side some of the native infantry were wounded. When the order to retire came the General Officer Commanding expressed to Major Browning his complete satisfaction with the work done by the battery. This gratifying news was passed on to Captain G. A. Jobling and Lieutenant J. Bury. The men reached camp very tired after their initial engagement and settled down again to the general routine of battery drill.

The next time the battery came to close quarters with the Turks the fighting was more severe. One morning early in March, about the time of réveillé (5 a.m.), rifle fire was heard. It was at first thought to be some infantry practising at the butts in rear of the camp, although it was unusual to begin practice at that time of day. Major Browning climbed up the embankment, and away on the desert he saw a force of Turks advancing towards them. The Lancashire men rather appreciated these surprises. The normal life of the camp had become dull; it was a welcome change to march against the invader; an exhilarating experience to gallop the teams into action and by the discharge of live shell to put to rout the enemy of the King. This was "something like soldiering." They never realised, when parading the streets of Church or Blackburn, or firing over the mountain range at Trawsfynydd in North Wales, that they were then preparing to fight the Turks on the Egyptian desert. One heard the clatter and jingle which accompany the saddling of artillery teams in preparation for action. Meanwhile the infantry had checked the advance and the enemy was retiring in close formation. There were about seven or eight columns of 200 men each, and as they hastily withdrew from the zone of fire they opened out and gradually increased their extensions until they were out of range. This was a rather curious procedure. Had the Turks greatly extended their lines, the serious danger to which they were now exposed from

Invaders put to Rout

shrapnel fire would have been removed. The gunners made a big demonstration. They fired altogether about ninety rounds, and when the battle ended the Turks were completely routed.

A few days later reports were brought in that there was another massing of troops for battle, and all arms of the service were ordered to attack. It is calculated that on this occasion we put about 8,000 troops into the field. The Lancashire Battery moved off shortly after daylight and brought the guns into action at a range of 3,000 yards. On this occasion the gunners placed their shells in the middle of the invading troops with demoralising effect. As the range increased the drivers galloped up with the limbers and the guns were rushed off to other positions offering a good field of fire. Here their "gun fire" (rapid fire) did more deadly work. The enemy was driven out of the ground on which he had previously massed his troops, and prisoners, stores, and a large quantity of ammunition captured. Before the troops returned to camp an aerial scout dropped a message to the effect that a big Turkish force was advancing against us from the hills many miles away. This message was carried by Battery Sergeant-Major Coo to the General, who ordered all the troops to camp. The battery horses were entirely exhausted after this long day, and a detachment of infantry was detailed to assist in pulling the guns across the desert. It was reported later that there were no Turks within 60 miles of the Canal. After this action Major Browning was again complimented on the efficient use made of his guns. All ranks of the Church Battery had done extremely well, and up to this time they had no serious casualties as the result of the fighting.

A few weeks later the Church Battery and a section (two guns) of the 6th (Burnley) Battery had landed on the toe of Gallipoli Peninsula and were climbing the rising ground above Lancashire Landing under the fire of our ships. They were on the road to Constantinople. The other six guns of the Blackburn Brigade were lying off Cape Helles, and were about to disembark when the order to "stand fast," which was almost immediately followed by another and final order, "Return to Egypt," reached them. Could it be true! Had not a mistake been made! Was it possible that the authorities would allow one battery and two guns of another battery and the Brigade Commander to land and send the remainder of the Brigade back to continue their sojourn in Egypt? The disappointed gunners reasoned together in this wise, and when the movements of the ship's engines set all doubts at rest, murmurings of dissatisfaction pervaded the company. It is not a custom of the Service to offer reasons for the promulgation of any order, and it is not for the men to reason why. But here were men who had been grievously disappointed. They had caught just a glimpse of one end of that tongue of land where was being fought one of the toughest battles in which British arms had ever engaged, and they had been living for days in the shell-rent atmosphere; they had seen visions and dreamed dreams of active service on the Peninsula; there was no body of troops more confident of adding further honours to those already won by the Brigade on the Suez Canal. And now they were steaming back to Egypt. All anticipations of a glorious life at Gallipoli were rapidly receding; what prospects of fighting did the future hold out to them? But amid all the disappointment there was one encouraging thought upon which to dwell. The Church Battery was on the Peninsula. There was not a man belonging to the six guns now returning to Egypt that did not wish the Church Battery "Good luck" and envy them their experience.

There were excellent reasons for turning back this half of the Blackburn Brigade and for keeping the Bolton Brigade on the Suez Canal. The troops on the Peninsula

Preparing for Action

needed reinforcing by infantry; the time had not come when all the Divisional Artillery could be usefully employed there. It was, therefore, decided that the wiser policy would be to keep the guns in reserve in Egypt, which was virtually the base for the Gallipoli campaign, rather than hold them in reserve on an already overcrowded strip of ground every inch of which was exposed to shell fire and which had to serve the combined purpose of advanced base, railhead for supplies, and general rendezvous.

The infantry trenches in Gallipoli were but a few miles from the place of landing, and the exposed character of the country deprived the artillery of any freedom of manœuvre. The only gun positions offering a good field of fire were just in rear of the trenches held by the infantry, and in the absence of natural cover gun pits had to be built and trenches dug for the men. For two days the Lancashire Artillery "rested" on the shell-swept base whilst Lieutenant-Colonel Birtwistle and Major Browning made a reconnaissance. On the third day a number of men were detailed to proceed by night to a given place in the battle area to dig gun emplacements and generally to prepare the place for the guns. During the next night the guns were dropped into the pits and trained on to the enemy's positions. An observation station was established with telephonic communication to each gun pit, and Captain Carus, of the Burnley Battery, went into the infantry trenches to observe the effect of the fire.

The battery was now seriously engaged with the enemy daily, and the nightly reports from the observation posts gave most satisfactory accounts of each day's work. Both officers and men displayed that courage and coolness under fire which are not expected from other than well-disciplined troops. The Burnley section commanded by Lieutenant F. C. Woodward had the first casualty in this fighting. The guns were being moved to one of the advanced trenches when Gunner Clegg was shot, and at night-fall his body was wrapped in a blanket and reverently buried by his comrades " within sound of the guns." In the big bombardment of the enemy's trenches in the beginning of June the Lancashire gunners did some excellent work. They served their guns amid a terrific fusillade of shell, machine gun, and rifle fire with a seeming indifference to the danger which encompassed them, and were most satisfactorily reported upon by the staff officers. In this engagement Sergeant Duckworth, of Accrington, was killed.

The most daring exploit of the Church Battery was when they took two guns up to the advanced infantry trenches so as to direct an enfilade fire along the enemy trenches situated just below Krithia. The men employed for this risky duty—a duty which does not often fall to gunners—realised the great personal sacrifice it entailed, but they never hesitated. Roughly improvised bridges were thrown across the infantry trenches, and at night the gunners silently crept across the ground. The men in the trenches were amazed at this procedure and quietly cheered them. A few hundred yards away field and machine guns were peeping through the loopholed fortifications that the Turks had set up, but curiously enough no opposition was offered. The Turks did not contemplate so daring a movement. The advanced position was gained, and the men dug themselves in. Lieutenant Bury commanded one gun and the other was in charge of Sergeant-Major Coo. The guns did some good work here. They made things very hot for the Turks and accounted for many casualties. Subsequently the gunners returned to their position behind the infantry lines. The Church Battery had suffered further casualties by this time, including Lieutenant Bury, who was shot when, in company with Sergeant-Major Wilkinson, he was making his way to the advanced observation post. The Lancashire Territorials

Mentioned in Dispatches

have done something to justify the artillery motto—*Ubique*.

Lieutenant-Colonel Birtwistle, the Brigade Commander, and Major Browning have been mentioned in dispatches. The Bolton Artillery, in the Suez Canal battle, was commanded by Lieutenant-Colonel C. E. Walker.

ROYAL ENGINEERS

Field and Signal Companies

THE Royal Engineers are the architects and builders of the troglodyte dwellings in which our army lives and moves and has its being. The " R.E.'s " are the handymen of the army. At one time they build up ; at another time they pull down ; they facilitate the movements of troops by removing obstacles that bar their progress ; they compass the enemy's destruction by preparing works of defence and sapping and mining his position.

Our troops to-day for their shield and defence rely upon the field fortification of the military engineer. With the introduction of firearms of greater precision and with a range extending from one mile to ten miles, together with the many other scientific devices which have rendered fighting above ground impossible except at the price of enormous slaughter—our soldiers have had to live and fight underground ; to burrow their way to the enemy. Instead of covering themselves with a sheet of mail as was done in earlier wars, they rely upon the scientific use of earthworks designed and built by the Engineer. These earthworks, in turn, have advanced in elaboration of detail, in the immensity and complexity of their structure and in engineering skill far beyond anything previously attempted in field fortification.

The East Lancashire Territorial Division is represented on the engineering side by two Field companies and a Signal company. The work of the Field companies comes

Sapping and Mining 29

under that comprehensive term, "field fortification." The Signal Company, a comparatively new, or perhaps it would be more correct to say a re-formed unit—is responsible for maintaining in the field effective communication between the Divisional units and the Headquarters of the General Officer Commanding. The guns in the field have their own telephonic installation, and observation posts are replete with field telegraph or telephone. Communication between these posts and the guns is established in rear of the fighting by parties of the Signal Company whose business it is to keep the Divisional Headquarters fully informed of all that is going on at the front by the reception and transmission of messages. The Signal Company is largely recruited from the telegraph department of the Manchester Post Office so that the telegraph section entered upon their active service with a professional equipment which, it is safe to say, could not be beaten in any similar unit in the army.

Field Fortification embraces all the measures which may be taken for the defence of positions in order to enable the soldier by the protection afforded to make the best use of his weapon. The Engineers do not, of course, belong to what is known as the "thin red line." Still they have to possess more than a nodding acquaintance with the rifle, because in an emergency they have to turn to that weapon to beat off an attack. The East Lancashires appreciated the protection the rifle afforded them when they were on the Suez Canal. But the Engineer is more often employed with tools—pick-axe, spade, crowbar, and other entrenching implements—and explosives. He spans the river with his pontoons, throws a ribbon of metalled roadway across the marshy plain, protects our front with a maze of wire entanglements, "traverses" and "recesses" the trenches to give cover against enfilade fire, builds sandbag redoubts, provides empaulments for the guns, and cover for machine guns. These are but a few of the duties done by the "Engineers of Old Trafford" (to give them their local appellation) on the Suez Canal and in Gallipoli.

When the Engineers reached Egypt in the closing months of 1914, they were immediately set to work on the Suez Canal defences, and the first casualties in the East Lancashire Division arising directly from the performance of military duty occurred in their ranks. In December 1914, in consequence of the bursting of a boiler on a steam launch, Lieutenant Wood and six non-commissioned officers and men were hurled into the Suez Canal and drowned.

The works of defence which Lieutenant-Colonel S. L. Tennant (the Corps Commander) and his men were engaged upon during their stay on the Canal were of an important and permanent character and cannot now be detailed here. Lancashire people, however, will be interested to know that the Engineers were specially commended by General Sir John Maxwell and that the Divisional Commander, in orders, praised them for their engineering skill. The Signal Company, commanded by Major A. N. Lawford (assisted by Lieutenant (now Captain) G. L. Broad), was also detailed for telegraph duties along the whole line of defence. While in Egypt the company was raised from a strength of (approximately) 150 all ranks to 208, and horses, vehicles, and general equipment were increased in proportion, and the Brigade Signalling sections commanded respectively by 2nd Lieutenant Newton (Lancashire Fusiliers); Lieutenant G. N. Robinson (East Lancashires) and Captain C. H. Williamson (Manchesters) were absorbed into the Signal unit, as it was believed that this would make for more efficient organisation.

The siege warfare in Gallipoli made heavy demands on the East Lancashire R.E.'s. Working parties were continually in the fire zone digging entrenchments, improving communication trenches, laying down or repairing telegraph or telephone wires, and making

The "Apricot Artillery"

bombs. When battles (like Mars la Tour and Gravelotte) only lasted one day there was little work for Engineers to do. The continuous and indecisive fighting of to-day is largely the result of contrivances of the military engineering art. The shells from enemy guns destroyed our defensive works, but the R.E.'s were always at hand with tools and equipment to repair the damage, and to give that technical assistance to the digging operations of the infantry for which they have proved themselves so well qualified.

In the action on June 4 the Field and Signal Companies specially distinguished themselves. Lieutenant Oscar Taunton, who died of wounds received during that engagement, was decorated with the Military Cross for checking the enemy's advance along a trench on the left flank which was exposed. With the use of bombs and hand grenades he held the position unassisted for two hours. Again and again he picked up the enemy's bombs before they exploded and threw them back again. For laying and repairing communication lines under heavy fire, Quartermaster-Sergeant Williams and Sappers A. Broderick (died of wounds) and A. Jones were awarded the Distinguished Conduct Medal.

The East Lancashire Engineers also helped to form the "Apricot Artillery." Our Territorials did not go to the Dardanelles prepared for bombing, and the Engineers included in their multifarious duties the manufacture of bombs. The shell had to be improvised. Fortunately the troops were well supplied with tins of jam, for these vessels, when emptied of their contents, were to be filled again for the Turks. One day the following order was promulgated: "Don't throw away empty jam tins. Collect them and hand in to the nearest R.E. depot." These tins were readily converted into bombs. Meanwhile sections were hurriedly instructed in the art of throwing dummy bombs until the "infernal machine" was issued from the Engineers Depot to be used with great effect against the enemy. These bomb-throwers were nicknamed the "Apricot Artillery."

Lieutenant (now Captain) G. L. Broad, of the Signal Company, was awarded the Military Cross for general service, and Lieutenant-Colonel Tennant, Second Lieutenant W. Allard, and Sergeant-Instructor Sowray were decorated with the Croix de Guerre by the French Government. The services of Captain G. W. Denison, the Adjutant, were recognised by his promotion to Major and his appointment to the command of a Field Company.

LANCASHIRE FUSILIERS BRIGADE

The Minden Boys

OMNIA AUDAX is the motto of the Lancashire Fusiliers. They earned it at Minden; they have vindicated their claim to it on the Gallipoli Peninsula, where both the Line and the Territorial Battalions have been represented. It had long been urged against the Territorial Force that the inequality of attainment in the standard of training was against the force acquiring the cohesion needed for war. It has now been demonstrated that semi-trained troops can, by a system of hard and continuous training for a comparatively short period, be moulded into first-class fighting men. When the Lancashire Fusiliers landed on the Gallipoli Peninsula they were true to their motto. They " dared everything."

5TH BATTALION LANCASHIRE FUSILIERS

(Bury)

THE Bury Fusiliers, commanded by Lieutenant-Colonel James Isherwood (who has received the C.B. for distinguished service in the field), sailed for Egypt with the other battalions of the Fusiliers Brigade, on September 10, 1914, and two weeks later (September 25) they reached Alexandria. Here they entrained for Cairo to take possession of the new barracks at Abbassia, and to begin months of strenuous training to fit them for the field of action. The Proclamation of the new Sultan, Prince Hussein Kamel Pasha, on December 20, brought early distinction to this corps. Colonel Isherwood was asked to furnish a guard of honour at Abdin Palace, and the company commanded by Captain W. Wike was detailed for this duty. The men were particularly smart both in their appearance and movements, and many officers of high rank personally congratulated Colonel Isherwood on commanding a fine body of men. These officers expressed great surprise when they learned that the Fusiliers were the citizen-soldiers of Bury, Lancashire, and that they were part of a whole division from that county.

On January 20, 1915, the battalion moved to Alexandria and returned to Cairo on March 18, to live under canvas at Heliopolis, and to take part in the review before General Sir Ian Hamilton, on Sunday, March 28.

Toward the end of April the camp was greatly excited. A rumour spread through the lines that the Division

Advancing against Krithia

had been selected by Sir Ian Hamilton to help him in Gallipoli. Officially, the men knew nothing, but the hurried preparations made by the staff, and the general interruption of the daily routine work, gave some semblance of truth to the report. The troops had become weary of the monotony of peace training and they welcomed the prospect of a more active participation in the struggle of nations. Why should troops whose watchword was *Omnia Audax* be confined to the Egyptian desert, fixing and unfixing bayonets as an exercise merely, and firing blank cartridges into the air instead of discharging ball ammunition at the enemy?

On May 1 a transport, with the 5th Lancashires and other troops on board, sailed for "Lancashire Landing," Gallipoli. On the night selected (May 5) for transferring the troops from the transport to the lighters and from the lighters to land, the enemy was replying vigorously to the fire of the *Queen Elizabeth*. The Bury lads marvelled at this, their first experience of a bombardment. They had got into the sphere of operations and they naturally wondered how long it would be before they were buried in a nullah or carried from the field on stretchers. But they were not in the least dispirited. Since they left home they had undergone a complete metamorphosis. They had put on the true character of the British soldier; their moral fibre had been materially strengthened; their physique had been greatly improved: they entered Egypt (comparatively speaking) as raw material; they came to Gallipoli the finished article. Consequently on the day of their landing they moved off to battle. The other battalions of the Lancashire Fusiliers had landed a few hours earlier and were already advancing against the enemy. The orders of the Fifth were to support the Rochdale Battalion (commanded by Lord Rochdale) and the Seventh (commanded by Lieutenant-Colonel Alan F. Maclure). The 8th Battalion (commanded by Lieutenant-Colonel

Fallows) was also engaged. The first phase of the battle was to deliver an attack with Krithia as the objective. The second phase was to take Krithia, and the third to capture the predominating position—Achi Baba. This latter position was stubbornly defended all day, and Krithia was strongly held so that no ground was gained. The machine-gun and rifle fire was heavy and effective, but the enemy's gunners were firing wildly and many of the shells did not burst.

The attack was renewed with increased vigour on the following day. The Bury men had to press forward against Krithia. Success meant gaining two miles of ground. The troops moved off about 6.30 a.m. and took up a position on the right of the 29th Division. The attack was timed to commence at ten o'clock. The Fusiliers were wearing the large helmets that had been served out to them in Egypt—excellent targets for snipers—and following the advice of their comrades who had been some weeks in this hard school of experience, this headgear was discarded. The attack opened with a terrific fusillade at the stipulated time and developed rapidly, but at the end of four hours' hard combat no ground had been won. The intervening space between our trenches and those of the enemy was simply raked with machine-gun and rifle fire. Nothing could live above ground, and there was no evidence of life anywhere, except in the flight of whistling bullets. The only place offering any degree of safety was close under the traverse of the trench. But to take shelter here would not take Krithia.

Colonel Isherwood decided that even at great sacrifice a movement against the enemy's position must be made, and simultaneously he and Major Wood, the adjutant, leaped over the parapet of the trench and called the men to follow them across the lead-stormed terrain. Colonel Isherwood never doubted that where he led, his men would follow, but the prospect of certain death in advancing over ground already covered with their own dead and wounded and a larger number of the enemy might, he thought, lead to some hesitancy. But the Bury men were not prepared to shelter all day behind earthworks. They wanted to take their share in establishing our command of the Turkish positions, and the only way to do this was to beat down the enemy's serious resistance.

Imagine the scene: The crouching troops with bayonets fixed and magazines loaded spring to their feet; they scramble confusedly over the parapet; their appearance denotes defiance; their movements, determination. A merciless rain of lead is directed by the enemy against this wave of courageous humanity. But there is no thought of turning back. The cry " Forward, my lads," is dimly heard above the rattle of musketry, and the men involuntarily raise a shout as they stumble among the dead bodies in the line of advance and fall into the advanced trenches, perspiring, breathless, and with an uneasy feeling that they cannot have faced that murderous fire unscathed. They had never before been so near the jaws of death. But all the men who began that fifty yards' rush (it seemed an endless journey) did not gain the trenches. In their comparative security the successful ones glanced along the line in the hope of finding comrades they now missed for the first time. But alas! their journey from trench to trench had not been finished. Some lay in the open, wounded and afraid to move for fear of drawing the enemy's fire; others lay dead, their hands still grasping tightly their rifles, and wearing the grim, painful frown on their faces like men who had fallen in the act of closing with their enemy.

The sacrifice which this brave and desperate movement had cost demanded a review of the situation, and Colonel Isherwood and Lord Rochdale held a brief council of war. They agreed to report to Brigadier-General Frith that in consequence of their greatly depleted line further progress at the moment was impossible. The reply from

Headquarters was "Stand fast until reinforced by the Inniskillings and the K.O.S.B.'s." Reinforcements arrive; the position is again violently attacked, and more men are lost. The brief rest afforded the men whilst waiting for assistance allowed their shaken nerves to settle down again, and when the fight was renewed they handled their rifles like men who had demonstrated their superiority over the enemy. But they never despised him. They had long ago realised that they were encountering a stern and stubborn foe; a bold, brave, courageous, daring fighter who would appeal to Allah and go to his death with that fatalism which seems to obliterate all fear.

The shadows of night brought an end to the fighting, and from a rough roll-call it was calculated that nearly 200 men had fallen. The risk attending any attempt to recover the wounded was great. Concealed snipers were waiting and watching for any movement outside the trenches, and they made no distinction between fighters and those whose mission was to succour the wounded and decently to bury the dead. Quietly a group of men with stretchers went in search of those who survived, and they turned over the bodies of the dead in order to collect the information stamped on the identity disc which hung round the neck of each by a cord. Writing home towards the end of May, Colonel Isherwood said that nearly all the casualties (200 killed and wounded) were attributed to the action of May 7, when they had to advance over a country literally swept by the enemy's machine guns and shell fire. "I think we were fortunate to escape so lightly, considering the heavy fire we had to go through. Several Regular officers from France said that it was a picnic there compared with what we had here on that day."

The next big advance was on June 4. The main attack was made by the Manchester Brigade with C and D Companies of the 5th Lancashire Fusiliers, commanded by Captain S. H. Milnes, on the left of the line, and A and B Companies in support. This detachment was commanded by Colonel Isherwood. Some brilliant work was done on this day. The Fusiliers and the Manchesters got close to Krithia, but the trenches that were captured had to be evacuated because the flanks were exposed to enfilade fire. Many prisoners were taken, including Turkish and German officers. They ran to our trenches with their hands held up indicating surrender. Their arms were collected and sent down to the base, and the prisoners were sent, under escort, to Alexandria. The trenches now held by our men were full of dead Turks, and the bodies of some of them had been greatly lacerated by rifle and machine-gun fire. The conditions prevailing are indescribable. Men had to be detailed to bury the enemy's dead. Before the burial party set about their task, the head of each was wrapped in a cloth well disinfected, and a ration of rum was their portion. The trenches were cleared after some hours of laborious and disagreeable work, but the intervening space between our own trenches and those of the enemy, fittingly described as "no-man's land," was covered with bodies in an advanced state of decomposition. It would have meant a great sacrifice of life to have attempted burial here. Swarms of flies were attracted to the stricken field, and this pest increased the casualty list by spreading disease. To the troubles of this time must also be added the serious pollution of the only available supply of water.

Two days later (June 6) Colonel Isherwood received orders to attack the vineyard on his right. The fighting was of a desperate character, but for a long time nothing could be done beyond holding the ground already gained. Eventually the Colonel sent a company under Captain Wike (who was accompanied by Major F. A. Woodcock) to press forward. The remainder of the Fifth proceeded along a line of trenches to secure a trench in the nullah from which to direct a heavy rifle and machine-gun fire.

The fighting that followed was very severe. The Fusiliers fought gallantly and lost heavily. Both machine guns fell into the enemy's hands, and the machine-gun officer—Lieutenant Geoffrey C. Kay—was wounded. Captains S. H. Milnes, E. F. Wrigley, and the Adjutant were also wounded. Meanwhile Captain Wike's company captured a trench at the point of the bayonet, but could not hold it, for they were literally enveloped in machine-gun fire. In withdrawing his company Captain Wike fell, wounded.

From this time up to June 22 there was the usual trench work, and further casualties were reported due to sniping. There was abundant evidence that the Bury men had accounted for many of the enemy. On June 22 the battalion was sent to Mudros for rest and to reorganise and re-equip. Whilst at Mudros Captain Paton, brother of Mr. J. Lewis Paton, High Master of Manchester Grammar School, was attached.

The Battalion with other Lancashire troops, on August 6 and 7, took part in some attacks which were intended to form a subsidiary part of one great concerted attack. Sir Ian Hamilton explained that Anzac was to deliver the knock-down blow; Helles and Suvla were complementary operations. At Helles the attack was directed against 1,200 yards of the Turkish front opposite our own right and right centre. Two Turkish trenches enfilading the main advance had, if possible, to be captured simultaneously, an affair which was entrusted to the East Lancashires. Again and again attempts were made to advance against the enemy's fire, and Sir Ian Hamilton said that our set-back was in no wise the fault of the troops.

" That ardour which only dashed itself to pieces against the enemy's strong entrenchments and numerous, stubborn defenders on the 6th of August would a month earlier have achieved notable success. Such was the opinion of all. But the *moral* as well as the strength of the Turks had had time to rise to great heights since our last serious encounters with them on the 21st

Desperate Fighting 41

and 28th of June and on the 12th of July. On those dates all ranks had felt, as any army feels, instinctively, yet with certitude, that they had fairly got the upper hand of the enemy, and that, given the wherewithal, they could have gone on steadily advancing. Now that self-same, half-beaten enemy was again making as stout a resistance as he had offered us at our original landing."

The enemy was full of fight and in great force, and success could only be gained after a great struggle. On the right and on the centre the first enemy line was captured, and small parties pushed on to the second line, where they were unable to maintain themselves for long. On the left the little ground taken had to be relinquished.

" But in the centre a stiff battle raged all day up and down a vineyard some 200 yards long by 100 yards broad on the west of the Krithia road. A large portion of the vineyard had been captured in the first dash, and the East Lancashire men in this part of the field gallantly stood their ground against a succession of vigorous counter-attacks. The enemy suffered severely in these counter-attacks, which were launched in strength and at short intervals."

The casualties among the Bury men included Captains Paton, W. C. Yapp, and E. S. Frizelle (killed), and Colonel Isherwood, who had taken part in most of the fighting since the landing in May, contracted illness and was added to the list of invalided officers. Practically his last act in the fighting area was to recommend three of his non-commissioned officers for promotion to commissioned rank. The day after these promotions were sanctioned two of them were killed. One of them was Lieutenant Whitham, who had done remarkably good work throughout the campaign.

6TH BATTALION LANCASHIRE FUSILIERS

(Rochdale)

LORD ROCHDALE's men landed on the Gallipoli Peninsula a few hours before their Bury comrades. This Battalion sailed from Egypt on May 1, 1915, reached the theatre of operations on May 5, and on the evening of that day were in the trenches before Krithia, once a collection of whitewashed houses, now a heap of ruins with the dominating hill Achi-Baba rising immediately in its rear. The passage from Egypt to the Dardanelles was uneventful, still there was plenty of life to interest the Lancashire troops who had spent six months on the Egyptian desert. The seriousness of their mission was brought home to them with full force when they approached the place of landing. For a long time they had heard the distant boom-boom of guns; they were now near enough fully to appreciate what is meant by naval supremacy. The guns were trained on the Achi Baba position and the Turks replied, but ineffectually, for all their shells dropped harmlessly into the sea. Some of them, it is true, got perilously near our ships, but happily not near enough to do any damage.

"We landed," writes one of the Fusiliers, "during a heavy and continuous bombardment. We reached the battlefield under the cover of darkness. As long as I live I shall not forget the experience. Our line of march was up the cliff and over some hills and undulating ground to the trenches. We each carried two hundred rounds of ball. With the break of day we received the order to advance and were met with a shower of shrapnel.

Facing Fearful Odds

We could not all live in these conditions, so that you will not be surprised to hear that the field was quickly covered with casualties. Some were killed; many were wounded, but we had not time to attend to any of them, for we were engaged in a life-and-death struggle and it might easily be our turn to fall by the wayside. How I got to the trenches without being hit I do not know. It was a miracle that any of us live to tell the tale. Captain Scott was badly wounded. The Turks, though bold and courageous fighters, do not like our bayonet charge. When we closed in on them they would throw up their hands and shout invocations to Allah, but we did not withhold the bayonet on this account."

Major W. D. Heywood also praises the fighting spirit of the Rochdale men. Writing home in the early days of the campaign he says:

"We are proud that the Sixth were the first battalion to get to the firing line, and I think it a tribute to the men that, taken as they were from peace conditions in Cairo and thrown straight in the firing line, they behaved so splendidly. They never hesitated to advance in the face of the machine gun and shrapnel. In the first day's fighting all the officers were splendid. Lord Rochdale and Major R. L. Lees and Captain Spafford (adjutant) bore charmed lives. They walked about as if on a parade ground. Captain Scott (wounded) led B Company with great dash."

Major Heywood said he would not forget in a hurry their first night in the trenches. It was an inky black night, and owing to losing their way they had to sit in a gully for two hours. Had the Turks known their predicament they could have wiped out the whole detachment with shrapnel. The bullets from the firing line were whistling over their heads. At last they got into a trench about 400 yards in rear of the firing line. The scene here was extraordinarily weird. Shells from both sides burst with bright flashes, and the coloured flare lights and the roar of the guns combined to make a fascinating, though terrible picture.

When the Lancashire Fusiliers Brigade joined the Mediterranean Expeditionary Force our troops had forced their way forward some 5,000 yards from the landing-place at the point of the Peninsula. Opposite them lay the Turks, who, since their last repulse, had fallen back about half a mile upon previously prepared redoubts and entrenchments. The situation when the Territorials entered the fighting area is best described in Sir Ian Hamilton's own words:

"Both sides had drawn heavily upon their stock of energy and munitions, but it seemed clear that whichever could first summon up spirit to make another push must secure at least several hundreds of yards of the debatable ground between the two fronts, and several hundred yards, whatever it might mean to the enemy, was a matter of life or death to a force crowded together under gun fire on so narrow a tongue of land."

Before this date (May 5) progress had been slow, and the fighting of a decidedly critical nature. We had made good our landing against a numerically superior force, and the fringe of country in our possession as well as the general character of that country made a forward rush imperatively necessary. Freedom of manœuvre was impossible, and many of the ordinary rules of warfare had to be set aside and the initiative of the General Officer Commanding relied upon to get over the extraordinary, the unprecedented difficulties in which our troops found themselves. The ground held was exposed to the incessant bombardment of well-placed guns on Achi Baba, and all the supplies both as regards ammunition and food had to come overseas. Troops usually depend upon the country they hold to provide a great deal of their subsistence. But this country was absolutely barren—a veritable wilderness. "The country is broken, mountainous, arid, and void of supplies," was the description Sir Ian Hamilton gave of it. The General adds:

"The water found in the areas occupied by our forces is quite inadequate for their needs; the only practicable beaches are small, cramped breaks in impracticable lines of cliff; with the wind in certain quarters no sort of landing is possible; the

Five Hours' Battle

wastage, by bombardment and wreckage, of lighters and small craft has led to crisis after crisis in our carrying capacity ; whilst over every single beach plays fitfully throughout each day a devastating shell fire at medium ranges."

This explains why the Rochdale and other battalions of the Lancashire Fusiliers were thrown into the fight as soon as they set foot on the Peninsula. There was no alternative to such a course of action, and as the other battalions of the brigade landed they, too, were marched against Krithia. On May 6 Lord Rochdale received orders with other troops vigorously to attack, for it was decided that ground must be gained at all costs. The men had to begin the engagement at eleven o'clock. Waiting for that hour was really worse than charging with the bayonet. There is little excitement crouching in a trench waiting for the impending fight, and it is not a good thing for the nerves. Presently the fateful hour struck and the dash was made. "Every yard was stubbornly contested ; some brigades were able to advance ; others could do no more than maintain themselves. Positions were carried and held, other positions were carried and lost." The gunners lengthened the fuses of their shrapnel, and their effective fire compelled the enemy to yield ground which our brave Rochdale men and their comrades took and held. For five hours the battle raged. Big guns, small guns, musketry fire, the bayonet, and the bomb were used in the contest, and both sides suffered heavily in killed and wounded. Hidden machine guns swept the Rochdale position and caused much havoc, but the men clung tenaciously to what they had won and were courageously facing the withering fire in order further to break down the enemy's power of resistance. But the French Corps had found a terribly hot corner—the enemy opposed to this Corps was well entrenched behind an earthwork and able to offer a severe check to our ally, who could not dig themselves in until night came on and stopped the fight.

46   6th Battalion Lancashire Fusiliers

The Lancashire Fusiliers began the attack on the following morning at ten o'clock, but the hidden German machine guns and the Turkish snipers hidden among a clump of trees made it impossible to advance without a tremendous sacrifice of life. The troops had been fighting continuously for five hours and were now exhausted, but they were not too exhausted successfully to assault the Turkish position at the point of the bayonet. They gained some 300 yards of ground and occupied the first line of Turkish trenches, which contained many dead bodies. At sundown new trenches were dug and the attack renewed the following morning. The Fusiliers were now withdrawn into reserve.

These initial engagements are tersely described by the soldiers as "hell." They claim that there is no other word known to them which so nearly applies to the conditions under which they fought. The Rochdale men had repeatedly to rush over an open piece of ground when the enemy's machine guns were literally sweeping the whole line with bullets (one of these guns can fire up to 400 rounds a minute, and the volume of fire is equal to the rapid fire of thirty men and very deadly), and the effective "bursts" of shrapnel were pouring showers of lead among them. But they never flinched. Every man of them went through this terrible ordeal with that bravery which will not accept defeat. They often essayed the impossible, and the death-dealing missiles thinned their ranks as they suddenly ceased their fire and rushed at the enemy with the bayonet. The word "advance" seemed to bring new life to the battalion. Men in various stages of exhaustion stumbled over the rough ground and fell upon the Turks with a spirit and dash which would have done credit to any of the troops on the Peninsula. Lord Rochdale had every reason to be proud of their gallantry.

"Bullets were whistling all around us and bursting shells added to the murderous fire," wrote one of the Fusiliers. "Our officers are a credit to England, especially Lord Rochdale, Captain Scott, and the Adjutant. There was Lord Rochdale giving his orders and saying, ' Give it 'em, lads ! ' and we were doing it for all we were worth. When night came and everything was quiet, Lord Rochdale said : ' Lads, I am proud of you. You have captured the hill ; you have done twice as much as we expected you to do ! ' "

Among the officers wounded were Captain J. J. Gledhill, Captain G. Scott, Captain R. W. Leach, Lieutenant L. Maurice Robinson, Lieutenant P. V. Davies, Lieutenant J. S. Berrington, Lieutenant M. C. De Wiart, Lieutenant J. S. Lord, Lieutenant T. D. M. Bartley, Lieutenant Eric Molesworth, Lieutenants J. and W. Taylor, and Lieutenant W. Redmond.

"We had an awful time," Captain Gledhill wrote from a hospital in Malta. "When D Company left the advanced trenches we met the full blast of the Turkish maxims, shells, and rifle fire. It was just like a hailstorm. Our men began to drop, but the rest pushed on. They did splendidly. They were followed by C Company (Captain R. Barker, of Todmorden, in charge), so you see the Todmorden lads were in the van. We left the trenches at 11.30, and I was hit at 12.15, concurrently by a machine-gun and a shrapnel bullet. My right arm was broken and badly shattered. . . . Here I am absolutely in the dark as regards the casualties among my men. I have seen no casualty lists, and I only hear fragments from some of my men who come to see me. . . . I learn that my company has been hard hit, there being only one officer left out of six."

Subsequently the Fusiliers had to repulse some severe counter-attacks. Occasionally the Turks effected a temporary lodgment and they were driven out by the bayonet. Every night up to June 3, assaults were made on the redoubt, and upon our line of skirmishers, but at the end our position remained intact. On June 4, the day of the big attack by the Manchester Brigade, and subsequent days the Rochdale Fusiliers were again in fierce contact with the enemy. The 6th Lancashire Fusiliers acted in conjunction with the Manchester Brigade, and took a prominent part in the capture and maintenance of the Turkish trenches.

After a fortnight's rest on the Isle of Imbros, they were back in the trenches on July 10, being in action for a third time a week later.

The worst experience of the 6th Fusiliers came on August 7, when they took part in a new offensive, which had begun the previous day with a fresh landing of troops at Suvla Bay. With others of the Lancashire Brigade the Rochdale men were ordered to engage the enemy's attention by an attack on the Achi Baba position in the south, while the new landing was pushed forward.

Of the fifteen officers of the 6th Battalion who went over the parapet to attack, eight were killed, six were wounded, and only one came back unhurt. The result of this attack was the capture of the vineyard by the 6th Lancashire Fusiliers, and despite many counter Turkish attacks, they held the ground till they were relieved some days after. This was the only ground that was taken and held at the Helles end of the Peninsula on this occasion.

Sir Ian Hamilton in the dispatch which covered these operations said :

"Both our Brigades had lost heavily during the advance and in repelling the fierce onslaughts of the enemy, but, owing to the fine endurance of the 6th and 7th Battalions of the Lancashire Fusiliers, it was found possible to hold the vineyard through the night, and a massive column of the enemy which strove to overwhelm their thinned ranks was shattered to pieces in the attempt."

Later, life in the trenches was not quite so strenuous, but the hardships of the campaign had not lessened. Bombardments were continued daily, and sniping and trench work kept the men busy. Amid all the deafening roar of modern battle some attention is paid to the spiritual welfare of the troops. The Rev. Denis Fletcher, the chaplain attached to the Rochdale unit, wrote home to say that it was impossible to hold church services.

A Mournful Christmas

To gather a big crowd of men in the open air was to invite attention from the enemy's guns. At one of his celebrations of Holy Communion his altar was two wooden boxes of provisions. The men knelt all round and the service was most impressive. "The men have to learn under these conditions that religion is a thing in themselves and that they must not depend on church or chaplain."

Lord Rochdale commanded the Lancashire Fusiliers Brigade in the engagement of May 6 and 7, and temporarily succeeded Brigadier-General Noel Lee in command of the Manchester Brigade. He was invalided home in October with typhoid fever.

On Christmas Eve the battalion left the firing line after a week full of excitement and danger. One of the enemy's trenches had been captured. During this exploit the Rochdales again showed the Turks that they were still full of fight, and that the bayonet was a weapon which they could use skilfully and with effect. That night they enjoyed the luxury of sleeping in hutments which were to be the winter quarters. Christmas Day was spent happily, though quietly. The rations marked it off from the ordinary day. But there were many vacant places; familiar faces were missing. It was known that some were resting in the new graves in the gully. They had made the supreme sacrifice only that week. Others had fallen in the fight and had been lost to them altogether. Christmas, 1915, therefore, was a time of chastened gaiety. Still, it is not well that the soldier on the battlefield should dwell on the past. Soldiers with drooping spirits cannot fight. It is right, it is fitting, it is indeed one of the characteristics of a great soldiery not to be insensible to the loss of gallant comrades. On the other hand it is fatal to success in the field to allow a feeling of depression to pervade the ranks. The Rochdale Fusiliers guarded against this. As the shadows of departing day crept over the stricken field there was a rattle of musketry. This stirred the men out of the reverie which a day out of the trenches had encouraged. The trench that they had captured in the previous evening was being attacked, and the battalion had orders to prepare to contest the right of ownership, when the firing became of a more desultory character and gradually died away. Presently a messenger brought the news that the trench had been vigorously attacked by the enemy and successfully defended by the 7th Manchesters.

There are many days in the life of our men on the Peninsula that will never be forgotten as long as they live. The Rochdale soldiers will always be proud of the fact that they were the first of the Divisional units to enter the fight. Boxing Day, 1915, will not be forgotten, for it was on the night of that day that the news of their early departure reached them. " The Battalion must be prepared to embark to-morrow," was passed from hutment to hutment and from man to man.

" The morning came, and the news held good," wrote one of the Sixth. " The Battalion was to move in the afternoon in full marching order. The day wore on, and before the time came the men ' fell in ' loaded up with equipment, oil-sheet, blankets, etc., and two days' rations. On the order to move, the first company filed into the gully and immediately went up to the knees in mud. It is not far from Eski Line to Gully Beach, but it took nearly two hours before the latter place was reached, such was the difficulty of negotiating the mud-choked gully. The ' dump ' looked strangely deserted, and that goal of the ambitious, the divisional canteen tent, was nodded a last farewell.

" The sun had set as we took the road along the shore. Imbros, a dark mass, was sharply defined across the water, while Samothrace, farther north, was bathed in the rapidly darkening afterglow. A few hundred yards were tramped, a halt was called, and the men, already somewhat weary with their heavy load, were glad to rest. Darkness fell, and the night grew chilly and cold, but no move was made for several hours. At ten o'clock we started again in file along the beach, picking our way gingerly over cobbles and wet sand. Soon we ascended the cliff and found a dull, smoky moon rising behind Achi Baba. Away back

Leaving "Lancashire Landing" 51

from the distant left came the rattle of the firing line. On our right along the top of the cliffs were the remains of the trenches from which a murderous fire had been poured at the first landing. Winding downwards, the base was reached at 'Lancashire Landing,' and another halt was called. Away over the eastward a flash was seen. A short pause; then, with a roar and a shriek, a shell hurtled overhead and struck the hillside just behind. A tremendous explosion followed, and showers of metal flew in all directions. It was 'Asiatic Annie' firing 8-in. shells from the far side of the Straits, a distance of five miles. At first it was hoped that it was an odd shot. But no; every ten minutes the flash was seen, and after about half a minute's interval the shell shrieked over. There was not much cover, but every man took what little there was and hoped for the best.

"This rather trying ordeal lasted until two o'clock, fortunately without accident, when word was passed along to file on to the lighter. From the lighter the steamer could be seen looming up in the dark a short distance out. The journey took but a few minutes. Officers and men soon settled down to sleep, and only one or two were aware of a shell that dropped half an hour later into the water a few yards from the vessel, and sending a column of water over the deck.

"When the sun rose the vessel was well out to sea. Away over the stern, bathed in a wonderful morning pink, was the peninsula, the place of high hopes, of disappointments, of sorrows and hardships endured, of danger encountered and duty done."

7TH BATTALION LANCASHIRE FUSILIERS

(Salford)

LIEUTENANT-COLONEL ALAN F. MACLURE took to Egypt and later to the Dardanelles a battalion of typical Lancashire men—soldiers every one of them. When in Egypt they developed those fine qualities which have since been so markedly displayed in the Gallipoli fighting. The Manchesters won great fame on June 4. The 7th Fusiliers specially distinguished themselves on December 19, a few days before the evacuation. Their gallantry on this date was specially mentioned by Major-General Sir William Douglas, and they received congratulatory messages from other officers holding high command. The details of these gallant actions as supplied to me by Lieutenant-Colonel Maclure are as follows: In front of our firing line was a huge crater formed by a mine explosion, which practically joined the firing lines. On December 19 we exploded a further mine, and increased the size of the crater, and blew in a portion of a Turkish trench which formed a loop almost directly in front. After the explosion we scaled with ladders the near lip of the crater and seized the far lip, sending bombers into each of the enemy's trenches right and left, and by this means driving them back. Our men, however, were driven out of the crater for a few minutes, but again regained it, Captain Boyd, who was in charge, carrying out his work most gallantly, as is mentioned in Major-General Sir William Douglas's orders and in General Sir William Birdwood's telegram.

Gallant Actions

The attack was made wholly by the 7th Lancashire Fusiliers. The 6th Lancashire Fusiliers were in the firing line, and gallantly supported them throughout. After the 7th Lancashire Fusiliers had taken the crater, the 6th Lancashire Fusiliers relieved them. The losses of the 7th Battalion were unfortunately very heavy. Amongst them were Major W. J. Law, the Commander, who was killed; Lieutenant Hartley, who was wounded and subsequently died from his wounds; and Corporal Downton, who had been awarded the D.C.M. for gallantry on June 4, 1915, and a bar to the D.C.M. for gallantry on this occasion. Private F. Mottershead was also awarded the D.C.M. for gallant conduct on this day.

Corps orders issued by Major-General Sir William Douglas, commanding the 42nd (East Lancashire) Division, dated December 20, 1915, were as follows:

"*Gallant Actions.*—The Corps Commander wishes to place on record the gallant conduct of the undermentioned officers, non-commissioned officers, and men of the 7th Lancashire Fusiliers in destroying the entrance to a Turkish mine shaft on the night of the 15-16th inst.

"On the previous night 2nd Lieutenant W. R. Hartley led a patrol with great boldness and judgment close up to the Turkish trenches and, besides other useful information, verified the fact that there was the head of a Turkish mine shaft only five or six yards in front of a crater occupied by our men.

"Captain A. W. Boyd, accompanied by Corporal W. Downton, Private F. Mottershead, and Private C. Bent, volunteered to carry out the destruction of this mine head. They carried a charge of 40 pounds of gelignite out and placed it in position without being observed. Private Mottershead, who had originally discovered the mine shaft, walked upright over the barbed wire to connect up the charge, which was successfully fired and completely filled up the entrance to the mine.

"This enterprise is only part of the good work that has been done recently by this battalion under the command of Major W. J. Law, and the keenness and energy displayed are deserving of all praise."

Major Law had taken over the command of the Battalion when Lieutenant-Colonel Alan Maclure was invalided. Major Law had already had his name brought before the Headquarters staff for his gallantry. He showed initiative and a contempt for danger which put heart into his men when the fighting was fiercest. He was always in the thick of things leading his men; encouraging them; urging them on to great exploits. By his own example he filled them with courage and cheerfulness when there was a tendency to be discouraged. When near the stage of exhaustion he stimulated them with the vigour he himself displayed and created in them a spirit of daring which at intervals seemed to be boundless.

Major-General Sir William Douglas, when he heard the news, wired:

"Tell 7th Lancashire Fusiliers that I deeply deplore Major Law's death. He has done gallant work throughout the campaign, and it is only to-day that his name and that of his gallant battalion were mentioned in Army Corps Orders for the good work done by them, thus adding laurels to the 42nd (East Lancashire) Division, which has already earned a great name."

Brigadier-General Frith said how much he deplored Major Law's death. He sympathised with the Salford men in their loss. "To-day's success has been due to his careful preparations and to the gallant way in which all ranks carried out his orders."

General Sir William Birdwood, "the soul of Anzac," after hearing of the repulse of counter-attacks, wired: "Well done 42nd and 52nd Divisions," and General Davies wired to the 7th Fusiliers:

"Hearty congratulations on your success yesterday, with many regrets for the death of your gallant Commanding Officer, Major Law, who is a great loss to the 8th Corps. I rely on you to hold the ground gained."

"Boyd's Crater"

General Sir William Douglas announced later:

" Permission has been granted to name the new crater which was the scene of yesterday's operations, ' Boyd's Crater,' in recognition of the gallant conduct and able direction of Captain A. W. Boyd, 7th Lancashire Fusiliers."

The experiences of the 7th Battalion were very like the experiences of the other battalions of the Fusiliers Brigade. From the time of their landing in May 1915 to December of that year they were trying to gain ground in front of Krithia. For days together they were in the advanced trenches watching day and night for any movement of the enemy, and sometimes relieving the terrible monotony of crouching under the traversed trenches by making a prearranged assault on the enemy's position. This subterranean warfare involves untold hardships. A sense of comparative security from the whistling bullet, the spray of lead from the firework effect of the shrapnel shell, the sweeping and withering fire of the machine guns, and the shell from a howitzer which is lobbed into a trench, may be disturbed any moment by a sudden display of activity on the part of the enemy. The 7th Lancashire Fusiliers had many surprises of this sort, and they initiated many surprises for the enemy. There was no rest day or night, week-day or Sunday, in summer or in winter. They were always filling and emptying their magazines; always keeping their eyes fixed on the earthworks that contained the enemy; often charging those earthworks, and at these times they placed complete reliance on their skilful use of the bayonet. The Turks are brave fighters. They are not living entirely on the fame which they won in the defence of Plevna. They showed a courage and endurance which the Salford men did not despise. But the bayonet charge was a too terrifying experience for them; they would rather face the bullets than the bayonet, and when the Salford men could not be checked by the infernal gale of countless shells and bullets they often took the line of least resistance and gave ground. But if resistance was offered the end of the charge was one of unspeakable sights and inconceivable horrors. But this is modern war, and the Lancashire Fusiliers were " playing the game."

The following are the principal events in the life of the Battalion in the Gallipoli campaign :

May 4.—Arrived off Cape Helles and disembarked early on the following morning. The Battalion was commanded by Lieutenant-Colonel Alan F. Maclure.

May 6.—The battalion moves up to the firing line to reinforce Lieutenant-Colonel J. Isherwood's (Bury) Battalion. The casualties on this day included Colonel Maclure, Lieutenant Kelly, Lieutenant Saunders, Lieutenant Brierley, and Lieutenant Usher—all wounded. At night the men link up the line of trenches to those held by the Inniskilling Fusiliers east of the Gully Ravine.

May 7.—Two attempts were made to take the enemy's position. In this engagement the Salford men were supported by the Bury Fusiliers and the King's Own Scottish Borderers. All the troops fought with great gallantry, although they had to face heavy shrapnel fire and the fire from concealed machine guns. At night the men were exhausted. For two days they had been in the trenches with little food, water, or sleep. They were accordingly withdrawn to a rest camp. The casualties were : Two officers and six men killed ; eight officers and 118 men wounded, and fifteen missing. The names of the killed and wounded officers were Captains A. C. Humphreys and R. Waterhouse (killed), and Lieutenants H. Broadbent, B. Shelmerdine, and R. R. Brewis (wounded).

May 12.—The Lancashire Fusiliers Brigade now worked in co-operation with its own Division under Major-General Sir William Douglas. The Fusiliers were the first units of the Division to land in the Peninsula, and formed part of a composite division in the early fighting. During

A Furious Cannonade

the night of May 11-12 the 7th and 8th Lancashire Fusiliers relieved the Australians in the firing line. There was a furious cannonade all day. For the next four days the Salford men were sapping and mining and protecting their front with barbed-wire entanglements. Casualties: three wounded.

May 16.—Relieved at night by the 8th (Ardwick) Battalion of the Manchesters. One casualty reported.

May 17-23.—Building wire entanglements, trench digging, road making, and performing other duties to improve our positions. Nineteen casualties.

May 28.—One killed and two wounded in moving to advanced second-line trenches. Engaged during the night digging a communication trench to Manchester supports. Constant fire from the enemy. Two men were killed and one officer (Lieutenant R. C. Woodcock), and eight men wounded.

June 4.—The whole line attacked the Turkish positions. Beginning at 8 a.m., our field guns and the guns of the Fleet bombarded the Turks for four hours. At noon, in accordance with preconceived plans, the guns ceased fire and a sortie took place. The Manchester Brigade occupied the central position, the 6th Battalion Lancashire Fusiliers under Lord Rochdale formed digging parties to convert captured trenches, the 8th Lancashire Fusiliers formed supports, and Colonel Maclure's men were in reserve. In this advance we gained 500 yards. At night the 7th advanced to the front line, but as they were a divisional reserve, companies worked independently and went to the assistance of other than Lancashire Fusilier units. Later the Lancashire Fusiliers Brigade made two support attacks on the Turkish trenches beyond the bifurcation of the Nullah.

June 10.—The Battalion was ordered to take up a position on the left of the divisional line. This was a difficult movement inasmuch as the men were under a heavy fire. They showed great bravery, and two of their number—Privates Casey and Downton—were awarded the Distinguished Conduct Medal. The casualties were: one officer (Lieutenant E. W. Roberts) and twenty-two men killed; seven officers and 138 other ranks wounded, and eleven missing. The wounded officers were Major W. J. Law (slightly), Captain A. M. G. Debenham; Lieutenants W. S. Scott, J. F. O'Grady, J. B. Leech, E. W. R. Field, and C. C. Fitzgerald, Medical Officer (slightly).

June 11.—From this day to July 13 nothing of supreme importance happened. The Battalion took its turn in the trenches and successfully met the enemy attacks. Subsequently the Seventh joined the 5th and 6th Battalions at Imbros for rest.

June 14.—In conformity with an emergency order received on the previous evening the Battalion arrived on the Peninsula to relieve the 8th Manchesters in support and redoubt lines astride the Nullah. Lieutenant Bennet Burleigh and seven men wounded. Lieutenant Burleigh died the next day.

August 7.—The enemy's centre vigorously attacked by the Fusiliers Brigade. The 6th Battalion was on the extreme left of the Brigade line and the Bury Fusiliers on the right. The two Salford Battalions were in the centre. The first objective was carried, but the two battalions on the right of the line had to bear the brunt of the enemy's attention and were forced to retire. Heavy counter-attacks were made on the line held by the 6th and 7th right through the day and far into the night, but they valiantly held their ground. The Turks did not succeed in dislodging them on the following day, when they were relieved by the East Lancashire Brigade. Four hundred and ten non-commissioned officers and men of the Seventh went into action; only 139 returned. The casualties among the officers were: Captain Blease (15th The King's Liverpool Regiment, attached) killed, and eight officers—Captains D. G.

Norton and R. H. Cade and Lieutenants R. R. Brewis, R. W. A. Usher (7th Fusiliers), and Lieutenants Wilson, Bremner, Bayley, and Morrison (attached from The King's Liverpool Regiment) wounded. Other ranks: forty-five killed, 141 wounded, seventy-seven missing. (The trenches gained by the 6th and 7th Lancashire Fusiliers were lost on the night of August 12-13.)

During the remainder of August and in September things were comparatively quiet for the survivors of the Seventh. Early in October ten officers from other units joined the battalion.

October 19.—A big crater known as Cawley's Crater, 10 yards in front of the parapet of the 7th Fusiliers, was loopholed and "sandbagged" by enemy during the night, in spite of our bombing and rifle fire. By means of rifle grenades and continuous rifle fire the Salford men destroyed the loopholes and subsequently made the sandbags useless.

October 23.—One man killed and six officers and two men wounded in consequence of accident with catapult bomb. This evening guns bombarded Turkish trenches immediately opposite firing position. Great damage done to their ramparts and barbed-wire entanglements. When guns ceased their fire enemy opened heavy musketry fire against our trench. We readily gained upper hand in this engagement.

October 27.—Turkish gun trying to silence a machine gun. Two enemy shells killed two men and wounded another.

November 2.—Major Law returned from hospital and assumed command. Battalion terribly depleted. Just able to find "fatigues" by utilising machine-gun section and Headquarters staffs.

November 9.—Major C. T. Alexander returns from hospital at Port Said and takes over command. Weather very much colder now. Periodically heavy rain. Trenches sometimes from 6 to 12 in. deep in water.

December 14.—Possess an advanced post in a crater. Observer actually lying on enemy's parapet.

December 15.—Privates Mottershead and Bent and Corporal Downton, D.C.M., went over our parapet to the entrance of an enemy mine shaft. Mottershead carried 40 pounds of gelignite, which he placed on the inner slope of their parapet. The men returned, the gelignite was dropped on the floor of the trench at the mouth of the mine and exploded by electricity.

December 19.—Major (Temporary Lieutenant-Colonel) Law shot through the head. Death instantaneous. Miners exploded two mines close by, and men jumped over parapet and made their way to far side of left ramparts. Working party followed. Three trenches entered. Cawley's Crater working parties begin consolidation. During bombardment Lancashire Fusiliers in the crater were enfiladed by machine gun, with the result that twenty-two non-commissioned officers and men were wounded and three were killed. Lieutenants Peak and Hartley were among the wounded. Late at night the enemy again attacked, and after about one hour's heavy fighting he was driven back. The machine-gun sections were in contact with the enemy all night.

December 20.—Heavy gun fire further thinned our ranks. Five non-commissioned officers and men were killed and eleven wounded. Lieutenant Hartley died. The command of the Battalion (or what remained of it) devolved upon Captain Gledhill (Adjutant). Furious bombing. We advanced on both sides of an enemy loop trench, barricaded and held it. The General Officer Commanding 8th Army Corps telegraphed congratulations to Captain Boyd on obtaining possession of the craters, and added that to perpetuate the event the new crater should hereafter be designated " Boyd's Crater." The General Officer Commanding 8th Army Corps and General Sir William Douglas, General Officer Commanding 42nd (East Lancashire) Division congratulated the

The Evacuation

7th Lancashire Fusiliers on their magnificent work; referred in terms of the highest praise to the gallantry and leadership of Major Law and deplored his death. Lieutenant Balmforth wounded.

December 21.—Three men killed, one died of wounds, and nine non-commissioned officers and men wounded. Enemy placed a considerable number of 8-in. (high explosive) shells near the craters and our lines, causing three casualties. Enemy also dropped about one hundred "whizz-bangs" on "Diggle Street" and "Ashton Road." Very heavy rain.

December 25.—Private Mottershead received from General Sir Francis Davies the following wire: "Hearty congratulations on your well-deserved D.C.M."

December 27.—Busy preparing to move. Left at night. Embarked in lighters at "Lancashire Landing" under heavy shell fire from the Asiatic side. One shell hit the pier. Fourteen officers (some attached, others recently joined) and 180 men left the Peninsula.

8TH BATTALION LANCASHIRE FUSILIERS
(Salford)

THE great fight for Achi Baba (June 4) was the first pitched battle in which the 8th Fusiliers were engaged, but it was not their first encounter with the enemy. For little short of a month they had taken their turn in the trenches and shared all the dangers and responsibilities of active service. How different it all was to what they imagined it would be! It was far removed from the simulation of war as practised by them on Salisbury Plain, on Laffan's Plain at Aldershot, or on the coast of North Wales. All the principles of war as inculcated in time of peace seemed to them to have been neglected or ignored. Instead of a pitched battle above ground in which all the science of strategy and tactics might have free play, the troops had "gone to earth." Skirmishing for position—short, sharp rushes to covered fire positions—an advance here and a check there—a deployment of this part of the line—the use of covering fire by the employment of special detachments—the hurrying up of reinforcements to deal with unexpected developments—the struggle for fire superiority; all preparing for the ultimate rushing of a position at the point of the bayonet—these were the main features of the battlefield as visualised by the Fusiliers. They had been taught to use the rifle with effect because it was upon that weapon that they wholly depended for success in battle. The spade, in their view, was quite a subsidiary implement of war. Indeed they barely recognised it as

Subterranean Warfare

a part of their equipment until they went to Egypt, and sandbags and other material used in field fortification they considered to be the stock-in-trade of the military engineer.

But in order effectively to use the rifle, they had in the first instance to use the spade. They had to adapt themselves to a kind of subterranean warfare. Manœuvre was impossible at any time, and movement above ground, even at night, was attended with serious risk. Sapping was their only means of " advancing an approach," and for ordinary trench work sandbag protection had to be provided. But with all the science and skill of military engineering the men soon found that they were not immune from the enemy's fire, and casualties were reported daily.

The 8th Fusiliers had greatly developed the soldierly spirit during their stay in Egypt. Lieutenant-Colonel Fallows, the Commander, following the principles and system of training which have made our soldiers such excellent fighters, had exercised his men to bear fatigue and privation cheerfully, increased their powers of initiative, of self-confidence, and of restraint, and produced in them a high degree of courage and disregard of danger, and thus prepared them, both mentally and physically, for the severe strain of active service.

When the time arrived for a bold offensive movement the Fusiliers were ready and eager for the fight. In the Achi Baba battle in the first week in June Colonel Fallows and his men were in the support trenches. For four hours they listened to the deafening roar of guns which, by way of destroying the heavy wire entanglements and earthworks, prepared the way for the infantry attack. At noon the guns ceased their troubling. There was an interval of comparative quiet. Then the ground dividing the trenches of the opposing forces became suddenly alive with a cheering, advancing line of Manchester men. They were at last making a move against the enemy's stronghold and hoped to get near enough to use the bayonet. These gallant lads had climbed over the parapet to the open field and were now facing a withering fire from the Turkish trenches, whilst machine guns on the left poured a heavy curtain of lead among the advancing ranks. Above them little puffs of smoke from bursting shrapnel completed the battle picture. The line became perceptibly thinner and thinner; the ground gained was strewn with dead, the dying, and the wounded. On the ground to be won a considerable number of the enemy had fallen.

At the appointed time the Fusiliers left their trenches and reinforced the fighting line. The Manchesters were now occupying Turkish trenches, which contained many of the enemy's dead and wounded. The supporting Fusiliers had to make their way across ground where rested many gallant Manchesters. The sight was enough to depress them. Officers and men laid there waiting to be carried away to a place which offered some cover from the devastating fire. The less seriously wounded attempted to crawl from the danger zone and to assist their more unfortunate comrades, but any movement was more dangerous than lying still. Not a few had received a fatal wound. The Fusiliers stumbled over the uneven ground and their fallen comrades, ever pressing forward against a formidable enemy who brought all his strength to bear against these indomitable troops who looked like storming his citadel notwithstanding the shower of lead now being poured among them. With the growing list of casualties they appeared to gather strength. Disclaiming the first instinct of nature—self-preservation—they were bent on doing their share to destroy that dream of conquest of the man who had set out with the idea of extending his empire in the blood of nations.

The result of this day's fighting was that the Territorials, who were in the centre of the line, occupied more ground than they could hold. The Turks fled when

Fighting in Shirt Sleeves

they saw the line of bayonets within easy reach of their trenches, but unfortunately some of our other troops had been held up by wire entanglements, leaving the Territorials in a dangerous position. For this reason a retirement was imperative or an enfilading fire would have decimated them. The 8th Fusiliers did not share the brunt of this fighting, but the part that was allotted to them was done in a way which entitles them to a share of the praise so generously given to all the East Lancashire troops engaged.

The 8th Fusiliers deplored the loss of several of their officers. Their popular Commander, Lieutenant-Colonel Fallows, Major E. L. Baddeley (second-in-command), Captain E. S. Humphrey, and Lieutenant G. A. B. Lodge were killed on the same day, and five or six were wounded. Captain Humphrey was shot through the head on June 5 whilst holding trenches that had been captured from the Turks on the previous day. He was buried alongside Colonel Fallows and Major Baddeley in the cemetery near the beach on Lancashire Landing.

The Battalion in the subsequent fighting was commanded by Major (temporary Lieutenant-Colonel R. D. Waterhouse). In the engagement on August 7, when Sir Ian Hamilton decided to launch an attack from Anzac and to deliver a holding attack from Cape Helles, the Lancashire Fusiliers Brigade was in the firing line. A stiff battle raged all day and here again the 8th Fusiliers had the misfortune to lose their Commanding Officer, who was reported wounded and missing. Other casualties among the commissioned ranks included Captain A. J. Goodfellow, another senior officer (died of wounds), and Lieutenant J. T. Littler (killed).

Colonel Waterhouse was last seen on August 7, when he was surrounded by Turks and fighting desperately in his shirt sleeves, in a trench from which the Fusiliers were compelled to retire. A little earlier in the day Colonel Waterhouse had been trying to take assistance to a party

8th Battalion Lancashire Fusiliers

of men of the Manchesters who were in difficulties. Among the rank and file, too, the Battalion's losses were heavy in killed and wounded. The Eighth, the youngest of the battalions composing the Lancashire Fusiliers Brigade, has done its share of the fighting—has borne the heat and burden of the day uncomplainingly. When Gallipoli was evacuated it was nothing more than a skeleton of its former self. Eight months' practically continuous fighting had caused deplorable gaps in the ranks. The only regret of the Salford men was that they had not left the Peninsula viâ Constantinople.

Through the kindness of one of the officers of the Battalion I am able to give a diary of the Battalion's movements and experiences during the campaign:

May 3, 1915.—Battalion left Alexandria for Gallipoli. Strength: 33 officers; 890 other ranks.

May 5.—Dropped anchor off Cape Helles. By evening of this day the whole Battalion had landed under cover of s.s. *River Clyde*, and was subjected to shell fire from the Asiatic coast. Dug-outs prepared for the night on Lancashire Landing.

May 6.—Moved off at 3 a.m. in direction of Gully Ravine and remained in reserve (under shell fire) until 4 p.m. At this hour—the machine guns had already gone forward into the firing line—A, B, and C companies moved out under a hot fire from rifle and machine guns to fill gaps in the firing line on the right and left of Gully Ravine. Part of D Company followed later, and the remaining companies were employed taking ammunition to the firing line. The night was quiet, and the men in the firing line dug themselves in. During the morning, when we lay in reserve, there were a few casualties from shell fire. Second Lieutenant C. H. Birch was severely wounded in the arm and side.

May 7.—Heavy rifle and machine-gun fire broke out at dawn and continued on and off all day. The enemy's shrapnel against our trenches was not effective. We

Heavy Turkish Bombardment

covered the advance of the 5th Lancashire Fusiliers with machine guns. At night-fall we were relieved by battalions from the 29th Division. On this day Captain A. Ll. B. Shaw was wounded but did not leave the Battalion.

May 8.—By 7 a.m. all companies had returned to bivouac on W. Beach. Our casualties were then given as 56. At 9.45 p.m. the Battalion moved forward to an advance bivouac on the Krithia Road.

May 11.—The Battalion moved up Krithia Nullah and took over some first-line trenches from an Australian Brigade. Our left rested on the Nullah. It rained and we were heavily shelled throughout the night. Our line was from 250 to 400 yards from the Turkish position.

May 12.—Bombardment at night more severe than on previous night. Captain A. L. Radford, of the 9th The King's (Liverpool Regiment)—attached—was killed.

May 14.—Fairly quiet day. At night scouts under Second Lieutenant A. C. Middleton went out in front of the trench and brought in Turkish arms, equipment, and clothing.

May 16.—There was a gap of 500 yards between our right and the French left. We moved out a covering party under Second Lieutenants A. B. Shearer and G. W. Sutton and our trench was extended towards that of the French.

May 17.—A battalion of the East Lancashire Regiment occupied this extension at 4.57 a.m. We were relieved at night by the 5th Battalion Manchester Regiment.

May 28.—Reached bivouac, and until June 3 were occupied in various fatigues—road making, trench digging, unloading ships, etc.

June 3.—We return to the trenches, two companies moving by Krithia Nullah and two by Achi Baba Nullah. We were subjected to heavy rifle fire during the advance up the Nullah.

June 4.—Captain M. G. Bird (attached to 8th Battalion Manchester Regiment) was wounded in the charge of the Manchester Brigade. After the Manchesters had gone forward the Battalion was moved up to occupy the trenches vacated by them. Second Lieutenant C. R. Boulenger was slightly wounded. Lieutenant and Quartermaster F. C. Slater was wounded when in Krithia Nullah.

June 5.—Captain E. S. Humphrey killed by enfilade fire. Second Lieutenant G. W. Sutton and Lieutenant R. H. Brewis wounded.

June 6.—Turkish redoubt on right of Krithia Nullah charged and captured by A Company with assistance of two officers and forty men of the 7th Lancashire Fusiliers. Casualties were heavy and included Lieutenant-Colonel J. A. Fallows, Major E. L. Baddeley and Second Lieutenant G. A. B. Lodge (killed), and Lieutenants John Wilde, E. H. Bedson (wounded).

June 7.—In the morning the enemy made an unsuccessful attack on that portion of the fire trenches held by C Company. Second Lieutenant F. B. Turner was wounded, but he did not leave the Peninsula. Second Lieutenant A. C. Middleton died from wounds received near captured Turkish redoubt.

June 8.—Second Lieutenant W. V. Boydell died from wounds received in attack on Turkish redoubt on 6th inst.

June 9.—Captain and Adjutant H. A. Kirkby was wounded in three places when in the fire trenches.

June 24.—Moved back to bivouac, where we were heavily shelled. Major R. D. Waterhouse and Second Lieutenant H. C. Speakman wounded. Major Waterhouse did not leave the battalion.

June 26.—Returned to firing line. Usual trench work and occasional casualties until—

July 9.—Sailed for the island of Imbros, where we remained until the night of 14th.

July 15.—Returned to trenches.

A Trench Captured

July 25.—Came back to corps reserve.

July 24, 25, 27.—Our bivouac heavily shelled. Evidence of augmentation of enemy's ammunition supply.

July 28.—Returned to trenches.

August 6.—Attack on enemy trenches by 29th Division covered by fire from the massed machine guns of the Lancashire Fusiliers Brigade and our rifle fire.

August 7.—Attack by Lancashire Fusiliers Brigade on right of Krithia Nullah. At 9 a.m. the 8th Lancashire Fusiliers captured a Turkish trench 300 yards distant from our firing line. They held it until four o'clock in the afternoon. The section of the trench occupied extended from the right of the vineyard to the "Dry Nullah." The Battalion was driven out by heavy Turkish counter-attack, and of the 340 men and thirteen officers who made the attack only two officers and about 80 men returned not wounded. The following casualties occurred among the officers: Killed—Captain A. J. Goodfellow, Lieutenant J. T. Littler, Second Lieutenant J. N. C. Morris (of 8th Fusiliers), and Captain Frankland, Lieutenant Tayleur, Second Lieutenants Deacon and Tucker (of 10th North Staffs, who were attached to the Salford Battalion). Wounded—Captain Whelan, 10th East Lancashires (attached), and Second Lieutenant Denroche, 10th North Staffs (attached). Major (now Lieutenant-Colonel) R. D. Waterhouse, who commanded the 8th Lancashire Fusiliers, and Captain Fischer, 10th North Staffs (attached) were missing. Lieutenant P. F. Arnold, who was in charge of the Brigade ammunition supply, was wounded.

About the middle of August the Battalion took over the trenches in the neighbourhood of Gully Ravine and was engaged in mining and bombing operations until the end of October. Second Lieutenant B. Horner was wounded on October 13. Lieutenant-Colonel J. S. Rogers (Reserve of Officers) commanded the Battalion from the middle of July until August 6, when in consequence of sickness he was succeeded by Lieutenant-Colonel Waterhouse. Colonel Waterhouse was missing after the engagement on August 7. The command then devolved upon the Adjutant, Major Kirkby, who had just rejoined. He held the command until September 22, when Lieutenant-Colonel Hardicker, of the 7th Manchesters, was appointed to lead. A month later Colonel Hardicker was invalided and Major Kirkby was again in command.

MANCHESTER INFANTRY BRIGADE

"They never Hesitated"

THE Fourth of June (1915) will ever be memorable in the history of the Manchester Infantry Brigade. The Manchesters on this day proved that they had been cast in an heroic mould. They faced fearful odds with a disciplined courage and an indifference to death which bordered on fanaticism.

The air was rent with the groaning reverberations of shells; flying messengers of death sent from machine gun and rifle thinned their ranks; bursting shells momentarily checked their advance; and yet, with bayonets catching the sunlight and throwing heliographic signals of defiance, they pressed on with a yell, and undismayed, through this " valley of the shadow of death."

When the roll was called the full extent of the sacrifice made was laid bare. Many names were called to which there was no response. Under the cover of darkness the bodies of brave Manchesters were recovered and reverently buried " within sound of the guns," and stretcher-bearers picked their way over the treacherous field, carrying with affectionate care their wounded and dying comrades.

5TH BATTALION MANCHESTER REGIMENT

(Wigan)

The Wigan men cannot be beaten at trench digging. It is in their line of business, and in their peace skirmishes at home they always showed more fight than the occasion warranted. When the " cease fire " sounded they used to blame the authorities for " spoiling a fight which had hardly begun," and they seldom hesitated to challenge their opponents to a hand-to-hand combat. For eight months the " Wigan colliers " have been on the Gallipoli Peninsula where the " cease fire " was never sounded and the fighting was continuous, but like the other Manchester battalions they have displayed the fighting spirit to a remarkable degree. No situation of danger seemed to check their enthusiasm, and their reserve of strength after days of exhaustive trench warfare and bayonet encounters made them a valuable contribution to Sir Ian Hamilton's army.

What manner of men are the Manchesters ? Shortly after the Boer War General Sir Ian Hamilton kindly sent me an appreciation of the work of the Manchesters in the South African war. In this appreciation there was a pen-picture of the heroes of Elandslaagte. This pen-picture also accurately described the heroes of Gallipoli :

"Your Manchester men possess, to my thinking, attributes which are clear cut and distinctive. There is amongst them an almost complete absence of military swagger or vanity or desire to show off. They suffer, indeed, from a lack of these showy qualities. They are not tall of stature, or exceptionally muscular

Epitaph for our Dead

or athletic—rather the contrary. It is only in difficulty and danger that the touchstone is to be found which can reveal to a commander the true mettle of the Manchester lads—their loyalty, their fearlessness, and their grit. In ordinary peace duties or in matters of camp routine they used not to be pre-eminent, but whenever it came to be a question of fighting they were all game—all without exception, strong and feeble, healthy or sick; whenever the alarm sounded the hospitals emptied, the depleted ranks were filled."

This is an excellent character from one who knows something about the fighting qualities of Manchester troops, and it is a great satisfaction to know that Sir Ian Hamilton has confirmed his early estimate of Manchester soldiers since his further association with them in Gallipoli.

After one of the big battles and a bayonet charge a soldier writing to his parents at Leigh asked this pertinent question: "What will Lancashire folk think of their 'Saturday afternoon soldiers' and the so-called 'slackers' when they see the list of casualties?" The people of Lancashire are proud of their sons.

Hear what a stranger has to say: "There was a great deal of apprehension in many a breast to see how they (the Territorials) would acquit themselves," said a writer in *Blackwood's Magazine*.

"They never did but magnificently all the time; and if there remain only a few battalions with even remnants of their former strength to show, it is because of the initiative they always took in those early days. They sacrificed themselves so selflessly that they were a constant inspiration to those who had borne the brunt since the day of landing, not excluding our French comrades on the right, who were manifestly impressed. We at Helles had the heavy end of the stick at this time, and it is the glorious and yet tragic index to the career of the 8th Corps that they almost invariably attacked and captured one more trench than they were intended to, with results that must often have been simply heart-breaking to our commanders. Every man who survives the Dardanelles carries in his mind the only epitaph there can ever be for our dead lying there between the fatal hill and the sea: 'They never hesitated.' One instance will suffice. It was the night after a big attack when the clear-eyed heavens looked down on simmering passions in that corner of the earth. The battle was not over; that much, at least, we could rely on. Any enemy movement, real or suspected, was enough to stir the embers of a bloody yesternight. It was real, as it happened—a pretty determined counter-stroke, heralded by vehement invocation of ' Allah! Allah!' It was delivered in a part of the line which was badly consolidated, but held stubbornly by the Manchesters. For neighbours, a little to the rear, the latter had the 5th Royal Scots, under Colonel Wilson, and when at length the onslaught by tremendously superior numbers drove the Manchesters back a little, no single minute did the Scots allow the advantage to stand. They were up out of their trenches with a yell that nearly the whole line heard, charging like furies ; nor did they breathe easy again till they had cleared every Turk out of our trench, which the enemy was just beginning to find very useful for bombing purposes."

Here is a further tribute from the sister service. One of the seamen on H.M.S. *Talbot* (a ship that rendered great service to the 42nd Division), writing after the battle on June 4, said that the Manchesters were taking a big part in the operations, and that the Manchester Brigade was making a big reputation.

"We in the navy are in touch with the army all the time, and can see what splendid work is being done. Besides supporting them with our guns we are doing as much as we can to supply them with any luxuries that we are lucky enough to possess. In the early days of the landing it was an inferno of shot and shell and the Manchester boys stuck it like sportsmen."

The Wigan men, with Lieutenant-Colonel H. C. Darlington (now on active service for the second time) as their leader, were not the men to falter in the fight. Immediately they joined the Allied camp on the Peninsula they shared the incessant toil and strife, " the trivial round, the common task." The day after their landing they stood, pick-axe in hand, waiting the order to break ground—to " dig themselves in." Under cover of night they crept stealthily over the difficult country, the eyes of a hundred sentries watching their progress and strain-

Facing Death Nobly

ing their necks to keep themselves informed of any enemy movement. Trench digging in the dark in an unknown country, within easy reach of the enemy, covered by his guns and rifles and exposed to occasional squalls of lead, calls for a sturdy and unbending courage. Physical and mental qualities of a high standard are needed to fit men for so hazardous an enterprise.

"Men fear death as children fear to go in the dark," said Bacon. But does this hold true of the men who fought in Gallipoli? Our soldiers faced death every hour —day and night—of their service there, and " they never hesitated." They showed a contempt for danger, and the ever-present prospect of death did not cause them to shrink from their duty. Invincible in determination, inexhaustible in resources, patient in fatigue, and bold in action. These were the characteristics displayed by the Manchesters, and to these sterling qualities are to be ascribed their great and glorious achievements.

The Wigan men moved forward to the fight fearlessly, and when hotly contesting ground with the Turks they almost invariably compelled the enemy to yield. Living for days in the cramped confinement of the trenches did not trouble them overmuch. It was the monotony of it that tended to depress their spirits. They had a consuming desire to "get at the Turks"; to have a clean straight fight above ground. "Let them come out into the open," they said, " and then we will show them what we can do. This peering at one another through sandbag loopholes is too dull a thing to be called ' action.' "

Now and again there would be some activity in the field, and the 5th Manchesters, in co-operation with their comrades, would be ordered to assume the offensive ; to advance their line 50 or 100 yards. Their objective might be a Turkish trench, or they might have to capture ground, hold it, and dig themselves in. This looked like asking for trouble. But the Wigan men were always ready for a desperate adventure, and they could be relied upon cheerfully to respond to the call of their officers. Colonel Darlington's men were in some stiff engagements in the latter part of May and early in June, and they gained a reputation for dogged perseverance. They never gained an advantage but they followed it up. Indeed, their excessive zeal often urged them to take more ground than they could hold. One cannot do other than admire courage, even though it be misdirected. It shows the right spirit, but it often tends unnecessarily to swell the casualty list and to perplex the leaders whose duty it is to hold their troops well in hand and to avoid " regrettable incidents." Heroic feats of this description must mean terribly depleted ranks. The Wigan men suffered greatly, but there is reliable evidence which points to even greater slaughter among the enemy. A state of demoralisation, too, was not infrequently noticed in the ranks of the Turks during the brilliant bayonet charges which were launched against them.

6TH BATTALION MANCHESTER REGIMENT

THERE is now nothing but a war-worn remnant of the original Sixth Manchesters. The first three months' fighting in Gallipoli reduced the Battalion from (approximately) 1,000 of all ranks to below 100. Ninety-three men answered the roll-call on August 7. The remainder of the gallant column had been carried off the field, some of them—their fighting o'er—to rest in a nullah just in rear of the ground they had so stubbornly defended; others, pierced by rifle bullet or perhaps cut and torn by shell, lingering between life and death, and now, for the most part, unconscious of the raging strife from which they have been withdrawn, to the dressing station and subsequently to the military hospitals at Cairo or Malta.

Amid the desperate and exciting business of a pitched battle—the deafening roar of guns, the bursting of shells, the explosion of bombs, the furious activity of machine guns, the rattle of musketry, the explosion of grenades; then the sudden lull in gun fire, the dying down of the musketry attack, followed instantly by charging lines of infantry, yelling and cheering as they madly rush across the fire-swept terrain—amid this hell upon earth there is no time to count the cost. Hundreds of men have fallen, hundreds more are dropping, and yet this devoted army of Manchester men never fails to hear and unhesitatingly to respond to the call of their gallant officers for further heroic efforts.

But when, in the comparative quiet of the night, the troops are withdrawn from the fire trenches to seek relief from the unceasing vigilance which is demanded of them in the advanced line, their thoughts naturally turn to the sacrifice this great ordeal has cost them. Many well-known faces are missing. Companies have lost their officers, platoon leaders are not to be found. Numerically speaking, what were companies are now only platoons, and platoons have been reduced to sections. The Battalion is but a remnant of its former self. An attempt is made to complete a roll of the survivors, and then something approaching the truth is known. A feeling of depression sweeps over the little company as they now realise for the first time the extent of their losses. They knew, of course, that they could not storm a strong position in the face of a tornado of shot and shell without loss. Did the end justify the sacrifice? They did not know the value of their work; what losses the enemy had suffered or how much nearer they were to their goal. What they did know was that they had given of their best to secure a victory and that it was with difficulty that their officers prevented them rushing into profitless peril. As it was they had to retire from the most advanced trenches gained. Then congratulations poured in upon the Manchesters. General Sir Ian Hamilton said that they had "done magnificently," and General Sir William Douglas could not find words to convey his gratitude to the Sixth Manchesters and the other Lancashire Territorials. Thus they were buoyed up with hope. Their brave ones had not died in vain. They had fought a good fight, they had finished their course, they had served their country well, and nobly upheld the honour of the regiment.

When the Sixth Manchesters left their home station for foreign service we little thought that they were destined for such great work. Officers and men we knew to be immersed in the military spirit; to be filled with patriotic ardour and anxious to march against the enemy. But how many of us who made any claim to express any opinion as to their fighting qualities entertained for one moment the belief that they would display such gallantry ; that they would show a heart for every fate, a willingness to submit to any loss and any sacrifice ? The storming, by the Manchesters, of the Turkish position before Krithia on June 4 will live in history. It will be one of the military milestones of supreme endeavour ; an illustration for all time of the military value and fighting qualities of the *un*-professional soldier. We do not forget the bravery of our soldiers in the assault of Badajos ; we cannot forget the heroism of the Manchesters and other of the East Lancashire Territorials in the " great adventure " at Gallipoli.

The Battalion went to Egypt (September 1914) under its Commanding Officer, Lieutenant-Colonel G. G. P. Heywood, who had the misfortune to fall sick before his men left for Gallipoli, and was subsequently invalided home. The command of the battalion on the Peninsula therefore devolved upon Major C. R. Pilkington, who was promoted to Lieutenant-Colonel. The regret felt by all ranks in consequence of the confinement to hospital of Colonel Heywood was tempered by the appointment of Major Pilkington as the Battalion's leader. The Pilkingtons, like the Heywoods, have a long and honoured connection with the commissioned ranks of the 6th Manchesters and neither officer could wish for a more devoted body of men.

The Battalion left Alexandria on May 3, 1915, and reached Cape Helles three days later, during one of the bombardments of the Turkish position. On May 7 Colonel Pilkington had orders to occupy the reserve trenches preparatory to going into the fire trenches on the following day. The 6th Manchesters, therefore, were engaging the Turks on the day after they reached the Peninsula, and on May 9 casualties among the commissioned and other ranks were reported. On each day in the month of May there was gun and rifle fire. Sometimes the desultory gun fire developed into a heavy bombardment, and attacks and counter-attacks followed. Trench digging, sapping and mining, and many other duties attending siege warfare were cheerfully borne; and officers and men were killed and wounded, especially in the trench-digging operations.

"On our way up to the reserve trenches we came under a perfect hail of spent bullets," said one of the 6th Manchesters. "They came all about our ears. I laid down in the regulation way (never more gladly), and pushed my greatcoat in front of my head. To lie still on the ground on a dark night, lead whirling all round, and no chance of replying, is most agonising and nerve racking. Three fellows were wounded round me and one ball dropped between my heels. However, we were to be tried more sorely than that. The order came round to dig trenches while bullets whizzed all around. This was carried out without a single casualty. The fellows behaved splendidly."

One night a detachment was ordered to take the place of the New Zealanders in the firing line. It was a miracle that the relief was not wiped out, for the guide lost his way.

"We seemed to come right near the enemy's lines, for all of a sudden a star shell informed the enemy of our presence. We dropped to the ground. A machine gun and thousands of rifles blazed away furiously, but their shots were high. Still the position was a dangerous one, and to extricate ourselves we had to make a rush for cover while this murderous fire was proceeding The miracle was that only six of our number fell wounded and that no one was killed. I rushed blindly into one of the trenches and was nearly bayoneted by the outraged inhabitants. I shouted out ' Friend, 6th Manchesters,' and was saved, but I was heartily cursed for jumping on some fellows who were sleeping. Another of our fellows jumped on to a bayonet which went through his thigh. It wasn't all over, however. Another field to cross under terrific musketry fire, and those fearful words ' Stretcher-bearers ' and ' Medical Officer ' ringing out now and again. And then we were in the trenches."

In the big battle of June 4 the 6th Manchesters lost eleven officers killed and ten officers wounded. Included in the list of wounded (and who subsequently died of wounds) was their Hon. Colonel, Brigadier-General Noel Lee, who commanded the Manchester Infantry Brigade. The 8th Battalion Manchester Regiment (The Ardwicks) in this engagement lost ten officers killed and about the same number wounded. In the first month's fighting these two battalions had lost practically all their officers. The 6th Battalion had twelve officers killed, one died of wounds, and nine wounded. The Ardwicks eleven officers killed (including their Commanding Officer, Colonel W. G. Heys), one died of wounds, and twelve wounded; or a total for the two battalions of twenty-three killed, two died of wounds, twenty-one wounded.

Captain J. A. Farrow, medical officer of the 7th Battalion Manchester Regiment, had his field dressing station just in rear of the trenches during the engagement, and was summoned by messenger to the support trenches when the Brigadier was shot. Captain Farrow found General Lee in the bottom of one of the trenches just in rear of the firing line. From this position he had been observing through field glasses the effect of the fire of his troops on the enemy. He had been appealed to by his brother officers not to take so many risks—to keep under cover and to make his observations by the aid of a periscope. But he was too keenly interested in his work seriously to consider any suggestions of this character. He seemed to have a contempt for danger, and was anxious to set a good example to his men. After he had issued his brigade orders he was continually visiting the trenches, for he liked to be in the thick of the fighting.

When dressing General Lee's wound a fragment of shell hit Captain Farrow, and although the wound it made caused him some pain he continued his attentions to the wounded officer. He took the precaution to remove to another trench, for he feared that the enemy had trained their fire on to the position where General Lee had received his wound. Captain Farrow had only just removed his patient to other cover when a shell burst over the spot vacated. The first dressing having been completed, General Lee was handed over to some stretcher-bearers, who received instructions to carry him back to hospital. Meanwhile the medical officer attended to other officers who had fallen. On his way back to the dressing station Captain Farrow saw General Lee walking to the hospital supported by the stretcher-bearers. When told that he was not in a fit condition to walk, General Lee wrote on a slip of paper (he could not speak) that he did not want to be carried off the field; he thought that he could manage to walk to the hospital. Before the journey was completed, however, he allowed the stretcher-bearers to carry him in a sitting posture, for the wound in his neck had made it very difficult for him to breathe. When in hospital an operation was performed, and he was thought to be making satisfactory progress towards recovery, but he could not rest. He left his bed and visited other officers of the Brigade in hospital, to whom he frequently expressed his desire to return to the active field.

General Lee had served in the Home Defence army for thirty years. He started as a drummer boy at Eton and was one of the few Territorial officers to reach the rank of Brigadier-General. During the training of his Brigade a few months before the outbreak of war he told me that he was attending his last training; that he would shortly retire. Three months later war was declared and the Territorial Army was mobilised. One night in August 1914, when the Manchesters were expecting the order to move for foreign service, he said (referring to his earlier statement as to retirement): "I have given up all thought of immediate retirement. I am afraid we are on the eve of a terribly big business. Even the youngest officer cannot be spared." Another fragment of our conversation I remember well. It had reference to his command.

Costly Bayonet Charge

"I have," he said, "every confidence in the Manchester Brigade. Whatever duty is appointed for it that duty will be done, no matter what sacrifice it entails."

Two days after the battle one of the wounded officers sent to a brother officer in Manchester an account of the extent to which the Battalion had suffered.

"Just a few lines to let you know what the poor old 6th have been through. I can't give all details of what happened, but we have been through a tremendous fight, and I should think one of the biggest charges of the war. It took place at midday on Friday, June 4, and our men went most splendidly, but the losses have been terribly heavy. I am sorry to say one hardly realises yet what has happened, but it is too awful to think of when one knows that all the following have been killed:

"Captains Bazley, Jackson, Kessler, Edgar, Pilkington, and Holt. Lieutenants Killick, Donald, Mills, Young, Compton-Smith, Brooke-Taylor, and Thorburn.

"Wounded: Colonel Pilkington, Major Worthington, Captain Davies, Lieutenants Aldous, H. C. L. Heywood, Collier, Molesworth, Hammick, Hellawell, and Blatherwick.

"All these casualties are up to Saturday morning, June 5, and I have not heard any news yet of Kershaw, although I have been told he was wounded, and Milne has put his knee out. Holberton (Adjutant), Wynne, and my brother were all right on Saturday morning, and I can only pray that they are still so, and we long for news. Molesworth and I are together on a hospital ship due in Alexandria this afternoon. I have a bullet in my left hand which is doing very well, and Molesworth has had a very narrow escape, but has got off with a scratch on his left arm and a flesh wound on his left cheek which has temporarily put his face out of shape.

"I can't write much more at present; one's mind is so unsettled at the great losses. I don't suppose 200 men stand up in the Battalion now. We have, however, upheld the name of the Manchester Regiment, and Manchester ought to be proud of her citizen soldiers when she hears what they have been through. All I wish is that I was sound and back with the poor fellows that are left, in order to try and help them through. I hope soon I shall be. Poor Donald was hit when getting out of the trench to lead his platoon in the charge. No finer way for a man to die. The C.O. I hear had a slight wound, but I believe was able to remain near the firing line. I only trust and pray that this is so. He is doing splendidly as C.O., and you know we are all devoted to him."

The trench is not an ideal place to infuse cheerfulness into the tattered remnants of a battalion. The excitement of the bayonet charge has passed away, and when the roar of battle has died down and there is nothing to do but wait for " the alarm," the men are apt to allow their thoughts to linger on the depressing side of their experience. This is, perhaps, more common among Territorials than among professional soldiers—men who have, as it were, surrendered themselves to the military life and through their constant training become more hardened to the grim side of war. The Territorials have shown that they do not lack courage. They are ever ready at the call of duty to submit to any sacrifice. The arbitrary claims of active service will not go unsatisfied where they are concerned. But there is just this difference between the Regular soldier and the Territorial soldier which makes the losses of the latter seem more severe. The Regular is, for the period of his service, wholly a soldier. He is, as it were, outside the civil sphere. The Territorial, on the other hand, was a free agent in so far as active serivce in the foreign field was concerned. In time of peace he is a civilian first and a soldier afterwards. He has come straight from his family circle, his business—he has torn himself away from civil life, and in many cases that was a severe trial, especially to the man with domestic responsibilities—for all the dangers, the hardships, and the uncertainties of active service. With their patriotism burning within them at a white heat the Manchesters deliberately volunteered for active service; they carried their civil and family ties into their military life, creating thereby that bond of fellowship which is peculiar to all Territorial battalions. They came from the same town, city,

Honouring the Dead

or village; they worked in the same shop or warehouse; lived in the same terrace. No wonder, then, that the sight of the stretcher-bearers slowly wending their way along the narrow trench with the body of one of their number (be he officer or private) tends to depress their spirits. They naturally feel a sense of personal loss, and nothing remains to them but to honour the dead hero with a salute as the body is reverently carried to a place of burial.

These observations will, perhaps, throw into relief the feelings of an officer of the Sixth who in a letter home wrote:

" There are none of us here who have seen war can ever desire another. I hate it and everything belonging to it. It all seems so inadequate that might should be right, or shall I say that right has to prove itself might to gain the victory? Very few can face such a crisis with equanimity. I cannot and never shall. Perhaps men who are born soldiers can laugh at death and revel in war; but I, who am only a poor lawyer who has temporarily doffed the robe to don khaki, must profess I prefer the robe. I do not say that I am not taking pride in doing my duty; I take an immense pride in my work because it is my duty and I like to do my best. But the work gives me no pleasure of itself."

One's outlook on life, even in war, is guided by one's earlier associations. The classical scholar cannot forget that he is on classic ground. The dawn and the sunset turn his thoughts once again to the Homeric poems. Nothing would be more acceptable to him than a copy of Homer to remove some of the weariness of trench life.

" I wish," writes an officer with a knowledge of the classic epic, " that I could describe to you the dawn and the sunsets here. It is indescribably beautiful. All the Greek epithets in Homer, like ' wine-dark ' and ' rosy-fingered,' mean here all they say. Please God, if I return home safely, I shall read Homer again for the sheer pleasure of realising to the full all that his adjectives mean."

A chaplain turns aside momentarily from the "horrible and loathsome" war to speak of nature's loveliness.

"The country here is gorgeous. Wild flowers of exquisite beauty, moorland and stream, and sea and trees, as beautiful as one could wish for, and amongst it all men killing each other. I buried one of the 6th Manchesters yesterday. He was shot through the head and died just as he was going to the ambulance station. There I buried him in one of those beautiful fields. He was only a lad, and in his pocket was a letter to his sister. There are no coffins; the body was just laid in the grave as he died. I put some of those exquisite flowers in his hands, and there he lies in his soldier's grave."

But in the midst of war's alarums and excursions the beauty of the landscape escapes the eyes of some of our soldiers. One officer wrote:

"One of the few saving graces of this beastly place is that one meets so many familiar faces from dear old Manchester. Words cannot picture what a God-forsaken hole this is.... Nothing but sand and rock and precipice."

After the big engagement on August 7 only ninety-three men were left to answer the roll-call. Referring to this engagement, Colonel Pilkington said:

"In the old volunteer days we used to say that the regiment would give a good account of itself when it came to hard knocks, but no one ever thought that the men would get so many hard knocks in so short a time as they got at Gallipoli. There was not a single man, however, who did not do his work thoroughly and well. I am proud of them. Everything was done cheerfully and without a murmur. On August 7 we were in the front trenches and about nine o'clock at night we were ordered to take a line 350 yards across. We got forward that night 150 yards in eight or nine hours, the Turkish trenches being only 300 yards away. That, I think, was the finest thing the regiment has ever done, especially when you consider that it was performed by men many of whom probably never used spades and shovels until the outbreak of war."

7TH BATTALION MANCHESTER REGIMENT

THE 7th Manchesters, in common with other battalions of the Manchester Regiment, wear as a collar badge that mythical monster, the Sphinx, to commemorate the campaigns of the British Army in Egypt in 1801 and again in 1882. But Colonel Gresham's Battalion has one distinction which is peculiar to that Battalion; a distinction which links it up with the Egyptian Army as no other battalion of Territorials is linked up with the Egyptians, for it carries, in addition to its own colours, the colour of the 7th Egyptian Battalion to commemorate —not a glorious war, but a glorious period of peace in that country at a time when the Battalion was preparing for that ever-memorable Gallipolian struggle.

Colonel H. E. Gresham, the Commanding Officer, was the Commander of the garrison at Khartoum during his battalion's service in Egypt, and the officers and men of this Manchester Battalion became so popular with the native soldiers that it occurred to the officers of the 7th Egyptians that the Manchesters should not be allowed to leave their country for active service without some outward and visible sign of the close attachment that had sprung up between the two battalions. No higher honour can be paid by one battalion to another battalion than this—to give its official sanction to carry its colour. At a big parade of troops this colour was presented to the Manchesters, and the Manchesters in turn had a replica of their own colour made and presented to the Egyptian Battalion. Whilst in Egypt, too, Colonel Gresham's battalion received another distinction—the acceptance by the Sirdar of the Egyptian Army, and Governor-General of the Sudan Administration—General Sir Francis R. Wingate, of the position of Honorary Colonel of the Battalion in succession to the late Earl of Ellesmere. The Manchesters won substantial victories during their peaceful mission, as they did later on the Peninsula battlefield.

The Battalion arrived at Alexandria on September 25, 1914, and reached Khartoum on October 2. Here Colonel Gresham and his men were met by H.E. the Governor-General, Sir F. R. Wingate, and the band of the 13th Sudanese Battalion played the column to well-appointed barracks situated on the Nile. Officers and men quickly settled down to their new duties, which for the most part were entirely new and often quite novel. The organisation of a camel company was an unthought-of contingency before Khartoum was reached ; it was soon an established fact. The officers appointed to this company were Captain C. Norbury (who commanded) and Lieutenants H. D. Thewlis and G. C. Hans Hamilton. This company made several long treks south of Khartoum. New country was explored ; interesting natives were met, and in the intervals " off duty " the men played football with the natives.

The presentation of a colour to the 7th Manchesters by the 7th Battalion Egyptian Army was a decidedly unique and brilliant ceremony. This was the first Territorial battalion to receive this distinction. On two occasions British battalions have presented colours to Sudanese battalions. In the year 1886 the 79th (Queen's Own Cameron Highlanders) Regiment presented a colour to the 9th Sudanese Regiment to commemorate the actions in which these two battalions fought side by side. In 1900 the 10th Foot (Lincolnshire Regiment) presented the 10th Sudanese Battalion with a colour to perpetuate their fighting at the battles of Atbara and Omdurman.

Ration Parties Predicament 89

Colonel Gresham accepted the colour on behalf of the Battalion and gave expression to the wish " that our united colours may always lead us to victory, and to the glory of our King and Sultan, as well as of the officers, non-commissioned officers, and men of our respective battalions."

On April 29, 1915, the Battalion received orders to prepare to move to the Dardanelles, and on May 7 it was off Cape Helles. On the evening of that day a landing was effected at V Beach, and after a march of two miles the men reached their bivouac. The subsequent movements of the Battalion, as recorded in a private diary, were as follows:

May 8.—Received orders to hold ourselves in readiness to support Australians who had moved out to fire trenches. The difficulty of getting water to the troops in fire trenches was very great. The Battalion had to find a party of men each with ten full water bottles to carry water to the front. This was a risky job, as they had to go over the open, as no communication trenches had been cut.

May 11.—Moved up to fire trenches and relieved the Wellington Battalion of New Zealanders. Access to the trenches was most difficult, as the Turks kept up continuous bursts of fire during the night. It was very dark, and it was not an easy matter to get the men safely over the open country to the forward trench. The Battalion was on the extreme left of the Division. On its right were the 8th Manchesters, and on its left the 89th Punjabs.

May 12.—When daylight came it was found that two platoons were missing, but fortunately they were found later in a support trench. They had lost their way in the dark. Owing to the position of our fire trenches it was impossible to ration the men during the day, and it was decided, when darkness came, to cut a communication trench. Information had been received that a bombardment of the enemy's position would take place for an hour, commencing at 6.45 p.m. At 7.45 p.m., when all was quiet, a digging party, a party with hot rations, and a machine-gun section with Lieutenant-Colonel Gresham, Captain P. H. Creagh, Captain C. Norbury, Lieutenants A. H. Tinker, Hans Hamilton, and G. S. Lockwood, moved off towards the fire trenches. Part of the way was by the deep nullah which runs north from Y Beach. The sides of this nullah rise perpendicularly, with small gullies running into it. Up one of these gullies, situated about 100 yards in rear of the fire trenches, the parties climbed to the open ground. When most of the men had filed out into the open a second bombardment began, in which the guns of the ships of both the British and French fleets and the artillery of both sides took part. Some of the men were able to scramble back to the mouth of the gully and get cover, but the larger number had to lie on the exposed ground for about an hour under a perfect hail of shells, for the position was such as to receive both the "overs" from the Turkish batteries and the "unders" from our own. This was the Battalion's "baptism of fire." In one small group of men, which included Colonel Gresham, Captain Creagh, and Captain C. Norbury, two men were killed and three wounded. The total casualties for the night were three killed and nine wounded. The maxim-gun section very bravely continued its way into the trench. As the rations had been scattered and great difficulty was experienced in bringing the dead and wounded down the gully and getting them back down the nullah, the digging had to be abandoned. The night was so dark that Lieutenant Lockwood, who had gone to reconnoitre a trench, in returning failed to see the edge of the cliff and fell some 30 feet. Fortunately he was not seriously injured.

May 13.—At daybreak food and ammunition were sent up to the fire trenches through the trench occupied by the 89th Punjabs. At 12 (noon) B Company, under Captain D. Nelson, made an advance in support of the

Trenches under Water

89th Punjabs, who had gone forward about 50 yards. In consequence of the intense fire of the enemy and the difficulty of digging in, this ground could not be maintained, and after seven hours' fighting it had to be abandoned. This engagement cost the company nine killed and twenty wounded. The wounded included Captain Nelson and Colour-Sergeant Combery.

May 17.—Captain H. Smedley reported gallantry of Privates Cunliffe, Thorp, Bramhall, and Taylor, and Captain A. E. F. Fawcus reported bravery of Private Frank and Thomas in leaving trenches and bringing in wounded under heavy fire from Turkish trenches.

May 18–24.—The Battalion was either in support or reserve during this period. The casualties up to date were 107, sixteen being killed. In the rear trenches casualties were always occurring from " over " bullets. In one day we had as many as fifteen wounded.

May 25.—Were ordered to relieve 4th East Lancashires in fire trenches, but owing to a cloud burst which flooded all the gullies, this relief could not be carried out until 8 p.m. Many of the trenches were full of water and fresh ones had to be dug. It was midnight before the East Lancashires were relieved. In moving up to the trenches men were up to the waist in water, and a very uncomfortable night was spent. The Mule sap up which the men had to proceed was at times a raging torrent, and men were almost carried away.

May 27.—Major J. H. Staveacre took over the command from Lieutenant-Colonel H. E. Gresham, who was invalided to Malta.

After the heavy rains of the night, May 28 broke with a clear sky. The Battalion was astride the Mule sap with the Royal Naval Division on its right and the Ardwicks on the left some little distance away. Captain Cunliffe, Lancashire Fusiliers (29th Division), was attached to the 7th Manchesters on this day to help them in the details of trench fighting. This officer's services were extremely valuable. The Mule sap all this time was a sort of mountain torrent and of little use, most of the men preferring to go over the top and take the risk of being sniped. Late in the evening orders were received to send two companies to reinforce the Wigan Battalion support line. B and D Companies went up and A Company took possession of the vacated trenches. C Company was already immediately in rear of the Wigan trenches. That night two companies (B and D) commanded respectively by Major (then Captain) Fawcus and Captain Smedley, went forward to the firing line with instructions to make an advance and dig themselves in. This was about as difficult an operation as could be imagined. The moon was practically full, the night clear, and the digging had to be done at a range of about 200 yards from the enemy. The companies passed over some unfinished trenches which had been dug by the Wigan Battalion, reached their line, and started digging to the accompaniment of a steady fire from the Turks. The casualties were heavy, but less than might have been expected. Altogether about sixty fell, and twenty-seven of this number were killed, including Captain R. V. Rylands and Second Lieutenant T. F. Brown. The length of trench to be dug—about 700 yards—was completed next day. The enemy's fire was again so accurate that a head exposed meant certain death. It was by so exposing himself that Company Sergeant-Major Arnot was killed. If anything Arnot was too brave. He seemed to despise the enemy. Meanwhile A and C Companies were busily digging immediately behind B and D Companies. These companies were pushing forward a communication trench, when Captain T. W. Savatard was shot through the head and killed, and a little later Company Sergeant-Major Cookson was similarly hit and killed. At night Lieutenant G. C. Hans Hamilton took forward his platoon and half of another to fill in the gap between B and D Companies, and on the

A Magnificent Advance

following night Second Lieutenant F. C. Palmer took up the other half of his platoon and joined Lieutenant Hamilton.

On the night of June 1 the Battalion was relieved by the 5th Manchesters and returned to the Redoubt line. The trench was by this time complete and joined up—a very creditable performance.

On June 3 the Battalion received orders for the launching of a big attack on the following day. The 7th Manchesters were allotted a position on the right flank of the Manchester Brigade. Their right rested on the Achi Baba Nullah and joined the Royal Naval Division. The first assault took place at 12 noon. This was carried out by two companies from each battalion of the Brigade. Colonel Gresham's men were represented by A and C Companies led by Captain C. Norbury and Captain B. Norbury respectively. These companies charged brilliantly over the 200 yards separating the Turkish trenches from ours and quickly captured their part of the main Turkish trench.

At 12.15 the second assaulting line went forward. The men were lined up ready in the first support line, and they had to charge to a supposed line of trenches about 300 yards in rear of the main Turkish trench now held by our troops. The remaining half of the Brigade took part in this advance, the 7th Manchesters being represented by B and D Companies under Captains (now Major) Fawcus and Captain C. E. Higham. B Company, on the extreme right, and one platoon under Lieutenant (now Captain) Chadwick was ordered to clear the Achi Baba Nullah and join up with the Royal Naval Division. D Company, on the left, was in touch with the 5th Manchesters. The advance, over a distance of 700 yards under heavy shell and rifle fire, was magnificent. The second objective was reached and was discovered to be a low bank—not a trench. Volunteers were now called to fill a gap between the right of the 7th Manchesters and the Nullah. These were quickly forthcoming, and as they manned their new line they were met by a large number of Turks led by a German officer. The Manchesters opened a heavy fire, and when they prepared to charge, the enemy, anticipating steel, hastily retreated.

Casualties now began to occur rapidly. Lieutenant Ward, and most of the men who had come down the hill to fill the gap, fell. The French and Naval Division were then seen to be falling back, and it was suddenly realised that the flank of the 7th Manchesters was "in the air," and that they were being enfiladed and fired on from behind. The order was given for the right flank to swing round and face the enfilade fire and to get what cover was available from a dry ditch and a huge shell hole running at right angles to the front line. The ground was covered with killed and wounded men.

The whole line retired towards evening to the main captured Turkish trench. The platoon commanded by Captain Chadwick was "held up" by a strong Turkish trench in the Nullah. It was here that Lieutenant Freemantle was killed, and Captain Chadwick and Lieutenant Hans Hamilton were wounded. The three following nights and days were anxious ones, as the 7th Manchesters and Turks were in the same trench. The Turks made several desperate attempts to recapture the ground they had lost, and the Burlington Street men had their first taste of grenade warfare. For the first few hours they were not able effectively to reply, for whilst the Turks had plenty of grenades the Manchesters had none. But the men worked splendidly. Despite their serious handicap they held their ground and consolidated it. Major Staveacre was killed while directing the supply of ammunition, and the command devolved upon the Adjutant, Captain Creagh, who has since been awarded the Distinguished Service Order. Two other officers who distinguished themselves in this fighting were Lieutenant

Reckless Bravery

N. H. P. Whitley (who in the retirement carried a wounded man to a place of safety) and Lieutenant Creery. Private Richardson won the D.C.M. for valiant bombing.

The casualties during this battle were about 250, including the following officers killed : Major J. H. Staveacre, Lieutenant A. E. Freemantle, Lieutenant H. D. Thewlis, Second Lieutenant L. Dudley and Second Lieutenant Ward. After a brief rest on the island of Imbros the Battalion returned to the Peninsula on June 23. During the battle on June 29 the 7th Manchesters were in reserve about one mile behind the firing line, and here suffered nineteen casualties.

By way of appreciating the work of this gallant Battalion, General Sir W. Douglas wrote on July 7 to Captain P. H. Creagh :

" MY DEAR CREAGH,
" It has been a matter of regret to me that so few of the gallant deeds performed by officers, non-commissioned officers, and men of the 7th Battalion Manchester Regiment are recorded. The cause, I know, is the lack of witnesses, owing to the heavy casualties sustained during the fighting from 4th to 8th June. If other heroic deeds during those days have come to light I hope that you will report them, though it may be too late for honours to be awarded.
" The dash, steadiness, reckless bravery, and endurance shown by the Battalion, and, indeed, by the Brigade, are worthy of the best traditions of the British Army.
" I deplore the loss of your Brigadier, General Lee, an able and gallant leader, who has given his life for his country. I feel sure that all ranks in your Battalion are imbued with a keen desire to avenge his death.
" Yours sincerely,
" (*Signed*) W. DOUGLAS."

Colonel A. Canning, who served in the Egyptian War in 1882, and came from the Leinster Regiment, succeeded Captain Creagh in the command of the Battalion early in July. The men were then engaged in constant trench warfare. The next big battle after June 4 was on

August 6–7. On the night of the 6th, about 8.30 p.m., two companies (A commanded by Captain A. E. F. Fawcus and D commanded by Captain Smedley) were sent out over the parapet to reinforce the Worcesters, who were believed to be holding a trench taken from the Turks. Neither officers nor men had any knowledge of the locality, and they were called on for this duty unexpectedly. These companies remained out until after midnight under a galling fire. It happened that there were no Worcesters (except wounded and dead) and no trench! After a long stand in a dip in the open between the Turkish and our own firing lines, Captains Fawcus and Smedley sent messengers back to report to Major Gerald B. Hertz on the situation. These messengers—Lance-Corporal G. W. F. Franklin (since commissioned as Second Lieutenant) and Lance-Corporal MacCartney—went back (each with one companion) with a message recalling the companies. MacCartney had already been badly hit in the arm, but he gallantly volunteered to return. Major Hertz tried to dissuade him, but he insisted. On his way back he was shot through the heart. Franklin got through. Captain Fawcus got the Military Cross for his cool leading on this occasion. The two companies lost about fifty men.

For the big attack on the following morning the other two companies were engaged. Captain Chadwick (who was wounded in the battle on June 4) took his (C) company first, and B Company (Captain J. R. Creagh) followed. The men had to advance out of a narrow nullah, upon which Turkish machine guns were trained. After the preliminary bombardment the 7th Manchesters emerged from their trenches and were simply massacred. None got more than 20 yards up the nullah, except Private White of C Company, who got through with a small party and remained under cover firing at the enemy until evening. White was awarded the D.C.M. for his gallantry. The remainder were either shot down or

Digging for a Comrade

remained prone till later, when they crawled back. Major Hertz took the responsibility for keeping back the next line of the attack, as any further attacking party would only have been similarly swept away. The gap through which they had to go only enabled two or three to go abreast. Captain Chadwick survived by a miracle. He did splendidly, and won the Military Cross for his work. His subaltern, Lieutenant A. H. Bacon, was killed, and Sergeant-Major Leigh was mortally wounded. There were altogether about sixty casualties, largely survivors of the British camel corps of Khartoum days. A few days later the Battalion had a short rest and then returned to the firing line. The usual well-known type of trench warfare succeeded, and except for occasional "rest bivouacs" continued until the evacuation.

On the evening of September 16 the Turks exploded a mine at the eastern "Birdcage." The 7th Manchesters lost thirteen men killed and nineteen wounded. There was much bombing during the night and some gallant rescue work was done. Private Moore went out to an advanced post and dug a comrade out, remaining several hours at work under heavy fire.

In amplification of the above I give the following narrative written for me by an officer who took part in the battle:

"The 7th were given a difficult nut to crack, viz. to attack the famous redoubt across the fork in Krithia Nullah in the first line of advance. About 120 men and two officers drawn from B and C Companies were detailed for the job. The lie of the country made a direct frontal attack all the way exceedingly difficult, especially as we had to retire to the 'duplicate firing line' during our own artillery bombardment and advance from there. The artillery promised to pay special attention to the redoubt and blow it to pieces. On this assumption it was decided that the most feasible plan was to enter the nullah from the 'duplicate firing line,' advance up it in single file, wheel to the right where it forks so that a left turn will get the party in line ready to rush the remaining distance to the attack.

"It appeared from observation that the party might be on 'dead' ground from the redoubt while executing this wheel, which was, of course, an important point. At the appointed time we defiled rapidly from the duplicate firing line and wheeled to our left up the nullah. We were, however, almost immediately spotted and subjected to heavy rifle fire and very accurate shrapnel. It was very evident that the enemy was prepared for developments in this quarter. The removal of our barbed-wire entanglements from across the nullah the previous night would have been noticed, but this was unavoidable. The advance soon began to get clogged. C Company, being on the right, had led off first. I was sent forward to see what was going wrong in front, for the men were round a bend out of sight. The trouble was immediately obvious; the heavy fire was taking its toll. The men in rear waiting in the open ravine did not know what was happening to those in front and were waiting for those 'crouching figures' to push on, and so let them get on in their turn. But many of these figures were dead. I pushed on till I got to the open corner of our own firing line, where I found some men collected who had lost touch already, and learnt that the leading men were on ahead with Lieutenants Bacon, Sivewright, and Captain Chadwick. It was obvious to me now that our attack had become disconnected; that for all useful purposes it had broken down. It was also obvious that I must advance and find out what had happened to the leading party. They had one—some say two—machine guns playing on that narrow gap between our firing line and the cliff of the nullah through which we had to debouch up the nullah. I remember that many things flitted through my mind in those moments, for I did not expect that many of us could come back. I collected together what men were there. We then dashed forward. I saw Sivewright, sitting, hit, against the cliff. I then came upon Chadwick. He at once signalled us to halt and lie down, and shouted back to stop any more men advancing. I threw myself down by him. He said it was quite useless waste of life. Our numbers were too small and the Turkish trenches were full of men.

"As we were in a fairly sheltered position—we were lying down at the bottom of the cliff—we dug in a bit and decided to remain, for although 30 or 40 yards from our firing line it seemed madness to attempt to get back just then. We (three officers and about ten men) lay there for hours, and when things got quieter we crawled, one by one, down the little stream, and were jolly glad to regain the safety of our lines again. Poor Bacon we left out in front dead, as well as a great many other brave men.

"Our plan of attack was based on the assumption that the

Disastrous Mine Explosion

artillery would knock the redoubt to pieces and also the trenches on its left which held a machine gun commanding the nullah. Our failure was due to experience proving the data worked on to be inaccurate. The redoubt seemed to be little if at all damaged. Its peculiar position made it a difficult target for distant artillery. It is believed that no troops in the world (of equal number) could have done any good had they been placed in the position of the 7th Manchesters on that day. The simultaneous attacks from the flanks fared little better, but there was some consolation in being told, after the fight, that they had magnificently attained the main purpose of holding the enemy troops to our front while the Suvla attack developed.

" It was consistently reported that at this time the Turks had actually massed on our front at Cape Helles a lot of their finest and freshest troops, and that they had intended to assume the offensive. There were several signs that this report was true. If it were true it is unfortunate that our troops had not learned the fact, for it would have paid us better to have been in the position to repel an attack."

The 7th Manchesters now returned to the ordinary trench life. They were only kept a short period in any of the trenches, because the physical condition of the troops could not efficiently stand the tension of the firing line for a long period. The beastly flies reigned supreme, getting fat and multiplying on the bodies awaiting burial, and on the food. During August and September there were many casualties from dysentery.

There was a big mine explosion in the middle of September when the 7th Manchesters were holding the barricade sector of trench across the Gully Ravine. It took place at the evening " stand to " and was in the first support line about 80 yards in rear. C Company had thirteen killed and eighteen injured. About 50 yards of trench had been blown up, leaving a huge crater. B Company took over the line, which was only 20 yards away from the enemy. All through the night the Manchesters were worried with bursting bombs and grenades. One grenade dropped right at the feet of Captain Chadwick and Lieutenants Pilgrim and M. Norbury, and exploded.

7th Battalion Manchester Regiment

Pilgrim was the only officer hurt. Captain Chadwick was also in the mine explosion and untouched. Two or three days later a heavy trench mortar shell was blown back over the trench by a strong wind. The shell exploded within a yard or two of where Captain Chadwick was lying. Several officers and a number of men were killed or wounded. Among the wounded was Captain Smedley, but Captain Chadwick was again untouched except for a scratch on his hand.

Major E. A. F. Fawcus, and Major and Quartermaster J. Scott are the only two officers of the Battalion who have the distinction of serving right through the Gallipoli campaign, whilst Major Fawcus is the only combatant officer who landed with the battalion and did not leave the Peninsula until the evacuation. Major Gerald B. Hertz, who was invalided for a short time in consequence of eye trouble contracted in Egypt, rejoined his battalion in the Dardanelles in the month of August and remained with it until the evacuation.

Colonel Gresham and Major Hertz have received a communication from the Sirdar (General Sir Francis R. Wingate) expressing his admiration for the fighting qualities of the gallant 7th Manchesters.

"Nothing," wrote the Sirdar, "can exceed my admiration of the magnificent behaviour of all ranks in the terribly hard fighting they have had. I deeply regret the casualties, but they have fallen in a great cause, and the Battalion has gained imperishable fame. I am indeed proud to be its honorary colonel."

I cannot leave the 7th Manchesters without brief reference to the Battalion newspaper, *The Sentry*, which has the distinction (among many others) of being the first all-British paper to be published in the Sudan. The paper is edited by Major Hertz. In the first number General Sir Reginald Wingate in a Foreword said:

"From the gallant Colonel downwards I know this battalion has leaders of the right sort who may say ' Come on !' but never

Fallen Comrades

'Go on!' and the men who follow them will go fearlessly forward to victory or death—death must come one day to all, and it has no terrors for the man who feels that he is doing his duty."

> " Conquer we shall, but
> We must persistently contend ;
> 'Tis not the fight that crowns us,
> But the end."

In the *Sentry* published after the evacuation of Gallipoli there is a touch of sadness. The first word is one of grateful remembrance of the officers, non-commissioned officers, and men who have fallen in battle. In an editorial note there is the following :

" As the traveller climbs up Bruce's Ravine from the shore of the Aegean, he will see deeply cut upon the white rocks on his right, among the ruder carvings of Gurkha warriors, the names of two men of the 7th Manchesters and our now famous Regimental motto, ' We never sleep.' He pushes on into the western Mule trench and enters a sap labelled with the familiar street sign of Greenheys Lane. Another hundred yards, and he is in Burlington Street, once simply the title of our own particular thoroughfare at home, but now known to every soldier who has served in the Helles area on the Peninsula. Such little marks and symbols commemorate for ever the part played by the Battalion in the great adventure of the Dardanelles."

8TH BATTALION MANCHESTER REGIMENT

THE heroism of the Ardwicks in that ever-memorable battle before Krithia, on June 4, 1915, furnished further evidence that the flower of chivalry still retains its freshness; that it is not preserved by us only as a specimen symbolic of a glory that has departed. Cherishing the great cause for which they were fighting; with a burning desire completely to justify the confidence reposed in them; determined to do their share in adding lustre to British arms; with an insatiable thirst for regimental honour and glory, they went calmly to their death. The efforts of the Ardwicks in this battle represented the highest standard of chivalry; after days of desperate fighting, their tired bodies sustained by an unconquerable spirit, they went forward and met a glorious end.

"It is possible," General Douglas wrote to the Battalion Commander after the action, "that other deeds of heroism during the fighting from the 4th to 8th of June by officers and others of the 8th Battalion Manchester Regiment may have come to light lately; if so I hope that you will report them. The dash, steadiness, reckless bravery, and endurance shown by the Battalion, and indeed by the whole Brigade, were equal to the best traditions of the British Army."

The Battalion left this country for Alexandria on September 10, 1914, with Lieutenant-Colonel W. G. Heys in command. During their training there the Battalion was quartered in Mustapha Barracks. Half the Battalion, under Colonel Heys, on October 20 (1914) went to Cyprus, the remaining half, under Major (now Lieu-

Gallant "Ardwicks" 103

tenant-Colonel) F. I. Bentley, staying at Alexandria. Colonel Heys commanded the troops in Cyprus, and took part in the memorable annexation on November 4, 1914. The half Battalion left at Alexandria devoted its time, with the remainder of the Manchester Brigade (the 5th and 6th Manchesters and one company of the 7th Manchesters), to training under Brigadier-General Noel Lee. In the latter part of January 1915 Colonel Heys and his men returned to Cairo from Cyprus for Divisional training. The 8th Manchesters were present when the Khedive of Egypt was deposed and the new ruler elected, and among other important duties assigned to them was the guarding of important works at Mex and outpost work.

In the first week in May the Ardwick men, with other units of the East Lancashire Division, were moving to the Peninsula. They landed under heavy fire from the Turkish guns and went that same night in support of the Essex Regiment, and four days later they relieved that regiment in the firing line, where they dug trenches and consolidated the positions taken. In the second week of war Lieutenant Johnson, the machine-gun officer, was killed and Lieutenant Morley was wounded, and in the subsequent fighting in May Captains Hepburn, Standring, and Lieutenant Scott were killed and Major Stephenson and Captains C. H. G. Collins (Adjutant) and H. C. F. Mandley were wounded. Captain Collins received his wound while carrying Captain Mandley to a place of safety. Captain Mandley had received a gunshot wound in his side and another one through his left hand. He lay wounded in a dug-out for ten hours under heavy fire until carried away by Captain Collins, who was wounded in the shoulder.

In the fighting on June 4 the 8th Manchesters proved themselves to be valiant soldiers. Orders were given for a general advance. The firing line in this great offensive was made up from right to left of French troops, the Naval Division, the 7th Manchesters, the 5th Manchesters, the 8th Manchesters, the 6th Manchesters, and the "incomparable 29th Division" and Indian troops. The Lancashire Fusiliers were in support of the Manchester Brigade. The objective was Achi Baba. Early in the morning (about 10.30) Brigadier-General Noel Lee, who had gone in to the support trenches immediately behind his troops to watch the progress of the battle, was shot in the neck. (General Lee died in hospital at Malta.) Colonel Heys, the Commander of the 8th Manchesters, was now called upon to command the Brigade, leaving Major (now Lieutenant-Colonel) F. I. Bentley in command of the Battalion.

All the morning the Turkish position had been heavily bombarded, and punctually at twelve o'clock the Manchesters jumped over the parapet and charged. During this desperate movement the 8th and 6th Manchesters suffered heavy losses. About four o'clock in the afternoon Lord Rochdale, the Commander of the 6th Lancashire Fusiliers, took over the command of the Brigade; and when Colonel Heys, Captain Talbot, of the 1st Battalion Lancashire Fusiliers, and an orderly, were going up to join Colonel Bentley in the main Turkish trench which had just been captured, all three were killed with shrapnel.

Here is the narrative of the fighting as told me by Colonel Bentley:

"The attack began at noon. The advance was divided into two lines, the first moving off just fifteen minutes before the second. The Manchesters went forward with great gallantry, and it was during their first charge that we lost so heavily both in officers and men. But nothing could stop them. The second line captured all before them. The 6th Manchesters, who were on our left, also pressed forward with great gallantry, and so the position remained until the retirement. First of all the French had to retire; then the Naval Division on our right. On our left the Indian troops and the 29th Division also retired, leaving the Manchester Brigade exposed on both flanks. Later on in the afternoon the 7th Manchesters had to retire, followed by the 5th Manchesters. This left the 6th and 8th Manchesters exposed to

Captain Oldfield's Heroic Stand

the enemy's enfilade as well as frontal fire, as they were the last to leave the ground, the retirement being made successively.

"Before the ground was evacuated, however, other troops—Lancashire Fusiliers and Engineers—came up to consolidate the position won. I received orders, at about 5.30 p.m., to let the men retire on to the main Turkish trench which we had captured, as no support could be given to them. In his dispatch Sir Ian Hamilton stated that it was difficult to get the men to come in. This was so, as they had advanced a considerable distance, and were certain that, if reinforced, they could hold on. During the afternoon one company of the 7th Lancashire Fusiliers, under Major Law, came up and rendered valuable assistance.

"About nine o'clock I got most of my men back to the main Turkish trench, where the late Captain Oldfield was in command. Captain Oldfield had been slightly wounded, and I suggested to him that he should retire for a short rest, but he refused to leave his men. At this time we joined up with the 6th Manchesters and the Lancashire Fusiliers and held the main nullah. I regret to say that early on the morning of the 5th June Captain Oldfield was killed.

"The fighting continued until June 8. In a battle of this kind it is impossible to see very much of what is being done by other troops. I can only say that the 8th Manchesters fought with wonderful gallantry, especially when taking into consideration that the majority of the men were fighting without officers, and in many cases without non-commissioned officers. We went into action with twenty-two officers, of whom ten were killed, the remainder being wounded. On June 5 none of the officers of the 8th Manchesters who went into action were left, with the exception of Captain Barlow, who was with the machine guns, and myself. The casualties, so far as I can estimate them, were approximately 500 killed and wounded.

"I cannot adequately describe the devotion and the bravery of the men I had the honour to command. Every man behaved nobly, and it is really difficult to single out any particular unit which did better than another. The medical arrangements, the commissariat, and the ammunition supply were perfectly carried out.

"As I stated earlier, it is impossible to describe the conduct of other units, but I feel that I should not be doing justice if I did not say that the 6th Manchesters also behaved with great gallantry and fought magnificently. Unfortunately these two battalions—the 6th and 8th Manchesters—suffered the most severely during that time, but all the battalions of the Manchester Brigade upheld the highest traditions of the regiment to which they belong."

8th Battalion Manchester Regiment

Captain Oldfield was the only officer left on the battlefield after the retirement. He came in with the remnants of his company (18 out of about 200) at midnight. Two hours later he was killed. One of the survivors of this brave little band—Quartermaster-Sergeant Fairhurst—who was with Captain Oldfield when he fell, in a letter home, gives a vivid word-picture of the desperate straits in which they found themselves. It reminds us of the heroic stand of the Manchesters of Caesar's Camp fame.

"We hung on like grim death to the ground we had fought so hard for till about six o'clock. By this time we had lost nearly all our officers, including the Colonel (Colonel Heys). Well, the order came to retire, and we retired steadily to the last line of Turkish trenches. I found myself in a kind of donga with about fifty men and Captain Oldfield, so I decided to stay along with him to hold the Turks back along the ravine. I little thought it a death trap then. About midnight an officer, Major Law, asked Captain Oldfield to lend him some of our men to help to dig a trench on our left and in front, so we let him have half of our little band of heroes. It left us to hold this place with about twenty-five men, Captain Oldfield, Sergeant Keeling, and myself. We had a terrible time after we let these men go. The Turks saw them leave the donga and gave it them hot. Well, we fought on like rats in a pit, and when dawn arrived (4 a.m.), we began to realise how we were fixed. We were cut off from all help. Then we lost our brave Captain Oldfield. He would insist on getting up to fire and exposing himself every time. I begged him time after time to keep his head down, or he would get one worse than he had previously got in his head, and which, I think, made him careless.

"We had been reduced to about twelve, and he was firing again—I had only just pulled him down—and a bullet struck him full in the face, and all was over. We were left now with Keeling in command, and we sent for volunteers to help us. But they did not get more than half a dozen yards before they were killed outright. As a last resort Keeling asked me to see if I could do anything. I thought my time had come, as I was a still bigger target than those who had gone on the same errand, so I bade our Jack 'good-bye' and made a dash up a communication trench that led up to the Turkish trenches, where I found some of our men snugly asleep while we were being murdered. But they couldn't assist, so I got down again and told Keeling, who had just been wounded, to hold a little longer till I got to headquarters, where I reported what was happening. Reinforcements were sent up, but our lads (about half a dozen) that were left had managed to get out some way, carrying Keeling with them."

The Ardwicks held their ground, although most of their officers had been killed or wounded in the attack.

"They withstood the brunt of the Turkish counter-attack which had repulsed practically every unit on the field, and held the positions they had won until the whole line some three miles long, already driven back, was able to reorganise, to go forward again some 200 yards, and to occupy the original Turkish first-line trenches. The 8th Battalion then retired to the new line formed, as it was found impossible for the remaining forces to advance as far as the position they occupied."

One of the bravest men of the Ardwicks is Private J. O'Connor, who was awarded the Distinguished Conduct Medal for gallantry in the June engagement. In a short appreciation of O'Connor's bravery, Colonel Bentley said how proud he was to have commanded the Battalion through the trying time of June 4–5. He was proud, although it was a sad time. Proud to know that even when his officers were swept down he had in the ranks men like O'Connor, who, without any hesitation, came down and asked if he wanted the wounded to be brought in.

"My men were absolutely splendid. They were prepared to take too great risks, and I had to check them. There were many brave deeds done in this war which went unrewarded. If O'Connor was asked if he was at all afraid he would readily admit that he was not without fear. The bravest man was he who, although he had a little fear, silently pressed on doing his duty, and with devotion and determination overcame that fear. That was what O'Connor did. To the front line, swept by shrapnel, the fire of snipers, and Maxims, he brought ammunition, carried wounded to a place of safety, and succoured those who could not then be removed."

EAST LANCASHIRE BRIGADE

Two officers of the East Lancashire Brigade have won the Victoria Cross, and in one case the gallantry displayed was of a quite exceptional character. Lieutenant Alfred Victor Smith, of the 5th (Burnley) Battalion of the East Lancashire Regiment, deliberately gave up his life in order to save his comrades from what must have been certain death. It was a fine example of the most daring bravery and self-sacrifice, and it is a matter of the greatest satisfaction that, as the result of an order issued by King Edward in 1902, the Victoria Cross may be posthumously awarded. Before this date, when soldiers or sailors had been recommended for the decoration but had died before its bestowal, the recipient's name appeared in the *Gazette*, but the Cross was never actually conferred. The decoration was never more deservedly won, and the parents of this brave officer will hold the highest decoration that the King can bestow in recognition of the highest and best type of chivalry. Lieutenant Smith slipped when in the act of throwing a grenade, and the missile fell back into the trench near his men. Realising the danger to which he had suddenly exposed them, he threw himself on the grenade and was instantly killed. Lieutenant W. T. Forshaw, of the Ashton-under-Lyne Battalion of the Manchester Regiment, won the decoration for gallantry in continuously bombing the enemy.

The East Lancashire Brigade is largely composed of men who were formerly employed in the cotton, the weaving, and subsidiary industries.

4TH BATTALION EAST LANCASHIRE REGIMENT

(Blackburn)

THE 4th (or Blackburn) Battalion was mobilised on August 5, 1914, and five weeks later left Southampton for service in Egypt under the command of Lieutenant-Colonel F. D. Robinson. In company with other of the East Lancashire Divisional units this battalion entered upon a strenuous course of field training at Cairo until the following April, when it moved to Port Said and relieved the Indian troops guarding the Canal there. Early in May there were rumours of active service, and on May 11 the Battalion had disembarked and was making its way to the advanced trenches to relieve the Howe Battalion of the Royal Naval Division.

Officers and men soon settled down to active-service conditions. In war, discipline is the first essential; and the first fruit of discipline is prompt, invariable, ready obedience to authority. In this as in other soldierly qualities the East Lancashires were not deficient. With good leaders they could be relied upon for any emergency. Heavily weighted with ammunition and carrying the equipment necessary for trench warfare, they entered the trenches and received the warm greetings of the Naval men, who, after several days on duty, had earned what rest they could get on the shell-swept base. The Blackburn men were at last within striking distance of the enemy. The relief had been effected; the East Lancashires were alone with the Turk, against whom they did not display that bitter enmity they had for the Hun. But " the Turk had seen fit to take up arms, and the Blackburn Territorials were there to show him how great a mistake he had made."

The fact that they were not far inland led them to ruminate on the task set the troops in that part of the great battlefield. Achi Baba dominated the surrounding country; to gain it was the object of their desire. Krithia, a ruined village, was but a stone's throw away. It was masked by the advanced lines of the enemy, and these lines were protected by wire entanglements and earthworks which the guns were intended to destroy so that the infantry might have a clear road to the Turkish trenches. The duty of the East Lancashires was to " hold on " ; to wait for the hour to strike for violent and heroic action.

On May 16 Major E. L. Carus and his men left their trenches at night and advanced some 50 yards towards the enemy's lines and dug themselves in. This operation made good the gap which had previously existed in the advanced line held by the Lancashire Fusiliers on their left and the French troops on their right. From now to June 4 it was virtually a war of attrition, and casualties were reported daily. Up to the big offensive on June 4 the Battalion had suffered about eighty-three casualties— thirty-two killed and fifty-one wounded. This was the first general offensive movement on the part of the East Lancashires, and in attacking the stronghold of the enemy they lost many men. But it is certain that the moral effect of this attack on the enemy was far greater than that of any success in the capture of trenches. The East Lancashires stood up to the enemy, and all his fine shooting from strongly entrenched positions did not intimidate them. Their object was to get to close quarters as quickly as possible, and by pushing forward to lower the fighting spirit of the opposition. This they managed to do up to a point. The musketry fire was gradually subdued and some bayonet work was anticipated. But the Turks fled. In the meantime well-entrenched enemy machine guns were doing their deadly work and concealed snipers were picking off both officers and men. Night fell on an undecided victory. Ground had been gained, but Krithia was still in possession of the enemy.

General Sir Ian Hamilton mentions the work of the 4th East Lancashires in one of his dispatches.

"For two more days his (Major-General Sir William Douglas's) troops were called upon to show their qualities of vigilance and power of determined resistance, for the enemy had by no means lost hope of wresting from us the ground we had won in the vineyard. This unceasing struggle was a supreme test for battalions already exhausted by forty-eight hours' desperate fighting and weakened by the loss of so many good leaders and men; but the peculiar grit of the Lancastrians was equal to the strain, and they did not fail. Two specially furious counter-attacks were delivered by the Turks on the 8th August, one at 4.40 a.m. and another at 8.30 p.m., where again our bayonets were too much for them. Throughout the night they made continuous bomb attacks, but the 6th Lancashire Fusiliers and the 4th East Lancashire Regiment stuck gamely to their task at the eastern corner of the vineyard. . . . By the morning of the 9th August things were quieter, and the sorely tried troops were relieved."

5TH BATTALION EAST LANCASHIRE REGIMENT

(Burnley)

THE heroic grandeur which characterises the sacrifice made by Lieutenant Alfred Victor Smith is something more than the culmination of many acts of bravery which specially distinguishes the campaign on the Gallipoli Peninsula. The standard of British chivalry has been raised by this unparalleled act of devotion; it is the refined gold of a war which (on the German side) has descended to the grossest barbarism. It is fitting that such intrepid virtue should be displayed on classic ground, and we rejoice in the knowledge that we can turn to this and other glorious deeds of our troops to redeem in some measure a war which for calculated terrorism and brutality has made " civilised warfare " little more than a euphemistic expression.

The Gallipoli campaign will live in history not so much as a campaign of disappointed hopes, but rather because of the great and unsurpassed heroism of the troops operating there. The 5th Battalion East Lancashire Regiment will share the immortal glory won by Lieutenant Smith. But its effulgence will radiate far beyond the regimental sphere, or the town of Burnley. As a nation we rejoice in the manifestation of such supreme courage and sacrifice, and we shall do well not to forget the spirit of self-immolation which dictated it.

Unsurpassed Bravery

Brigadier-General A. W. Tufnell, writing to the father, sends the following appreciation of his son's heroism :

"I did not know your son, as I only took over command of the Brigade about a fortnight after his death, but I have heard much about him and about his death, so, besides offering you my heartfelt sympathy in your loss, I can give you particulars almost as well as anyone else. He was employed in the trenches in Gallipoli at the time, and had just lighted a grenade for throwing himself. It was wet and slippery; he unfortunately fell, and the lighted grenade rolled out of his hand into the trench. Smith ran to take cover, as it was clear that the grenade must explode in a few seconds, but as he ran he evidently realised that there were many others, officers and men, in the trench, and that many of them would be killed or wounded by the inevitable explosion. His mind was made up in a moment, and without an instant's hesitation he ran back and threw himself upon the lighted grenade. Possibly he may have thought that he could still extinguish it; possibly he had no time to consider whether there was such a possibility; more likely he deliberately forfeited his life to save others from death and injury. Whatever his thoughts and decision may have been, his act was one of bravery such as I, personally, have never heard surpassed. There was only one result possible. The grenade exploded with all its force, and his life was sacrificed to save others.

"His name has gone forward with strong recommendation for the award of the Victoria Cross, which is the highest aim of every soldier, and at the present of nearly every gentleman of Britain, and I hope with all my heart that his gallant action may receive this highest recognition which it merits. I am afraid no decoration can compensate for the loss of an only son, but my explanation must be a consolation to you in itself, and, if the hopes which I have outlined are realised, it must make you one of the proudest men in England, when everyone reads the story and couples the memory of his name with that old and honoured phrase, ' A soldier and a gentleman.' I cannot close without assuring you that the admiration expressed in these lines is not mine alone, but the thought of every officer, non-commissioned officer, and man in the brigade which I have the honour to command."

The Burnley Territorials left this country for Imperial service with the other Divisional units, five weeks after the outbreak of war. After training in Egypt they joined (May 1915) the troops on the Gallipoli Peninsula which were badly in need of reinforcements. Once they set foot on the Peninsula they were under fire, and it was only when they went to Imbros or some other adjacent island that they could get free of the nerve-shattering bombardment and the horrors, privations, and pestilence which at the time of their landing were inseparably associated with the fighting. The condition of the field during the warm summer, together with the exceptional character of the operations, involving crowded quarters, unusual exertion of body, anxiety of mind, and the impossibility of recruiting their exhausted strength by needful rest at the base, which was almost incessantly bombarded, and where every hour their sleep was broken by the bursting of shells and the explosion of mines—was a test of endurance which few campaigns of the past have demanded of the best-trained professional troops. There was no respite, either by day or by night. The Turks were offering a stubborn and apparently unsubdued resistance. We had taken the field with every advantage of well-armed and disciplined troops, but they had to contend with untold disadvantages. What the Burnley men regarded as the hardest condition of all was to be standing in the trenches—neither gaining ground nor losing it—and to see their comrades fall. Although their casualties were not heavy they were regular ; the depleting process was going on all the time, and they had little or no redress. Their bayonets were thirsting for blood ; their magazines were hungering to be emptied on the ranks of the Ottoman Army. Now and again they did inflict material damage on the enemy. Sometimes they forced him back at the point of the bayonet, but the Turk did not wait for the steel. He preferred to run away and to renew the fight at a more convenient time.

Individual instances of bravery have been brought to notice through the medium of letters. An officer, re-

Captain H. Bolton Killed

ferring to the death of Captain Hargreaves Bolton, who was shot through the head during an advance, says :

" He lived for a few hours, out of reach of any help, though one of the men risked his life and crept in to let us know of his officer's condition. Captain Bolton went out with the first party on the first day of the advance. He returned twice to see about his men. He was told that he was foolish, but he said, in his usual deliberate manner, ' I wanted to know if they were all right.' He went out again and got safely dug in. Once or twice I have heard that his men cautioned him to be careful, but he was so devoted to duty that he was constantly looking out to see that his men were safe. He was also on the look-out for snipers, and was using his periscope, but he must have exposed his head too much. His brother John asked permission to go out to him, but was told that one catastrophe was enough. Almost every man in Captain Bolton's company would have gone out to him had they been permitted, they loved him so. He was always doing something to help them—a man slow to anger, of mature judgment, a man who not only made the best of things, but thought the best of everyone."

Captain Charles G. Lutyens, an officer of the 2nd Battalion of the East Lancashire Regiment, displayed great gallantry in quite exceptional circumstances, at Anzac. Captain Lutyens was at home on leave from South Africa when the war broke out. His regiment had gone to France and he was posted to a company of the 6th East Lancashires for service in Gallipoli. He landed at Anzac on August 4, and went in support of the Australians in the severe fighting of that time. He was wounded in the leg shortly after landing. On the evening of August 8 he lay under heavy shell fire in a dug-out, with Second Lieutenant P. L. Bathurst, his junior subaltern and only officer. He was very ill with dysentery. He said to Lieutenant Bathurst, " I will go to this scrap to-morrow if I have to go on my hands and knees." The regiment marched all night. At daybreak Captain Lutyens and his company were the first to reach the rendezvous. The Colonel and Major were waiting for the remaining companies of the Battalion to come up when the General ordered an immediate attack. The Colonel begged to be allowed to wait till the regiment got up, but the General repeated the order, and the Colonel turned to Captain Lutyens, and said, "Good-bye, old chap, I am afraid you are in for a tough job." The company went forward and rushed Rhododendron Spur at the point of the bayonet. Captain Lutyens was shot through the wrist, but taking his revolver in his left hand he led his men forward. He had not gone far before he was mortally wounded. He was carried past his Colonel and Major "cheerful and happy." Before the other companies of the Battalion arrived on the ground the Colonel was killed and the Major was badly wounded in the head. Captain Lutyens was a great-grand-nephew to Captain Engelbert Lutyens, 20th Foot (Lancashire Fusiliers), who had charge of Napoleon at St. Helena, and of Major Benjamin Lutyens, 10th Hussars, who was A.D.C. to Sir John Moore at Corunna.

9TH BATTALION MANCHESTER REGIMENT
(Ashton)

THE Ashton-under-Lyne and Oldham Territorial Battalions are still officially known as units of the Manchester Regiment. Under the Volunteer Regulations battalions were raised without regard to the higher formations and the due proportion of infantry to the other arms of the service as obtains in the Regular Army. The introduction of the Territorial organisation altered all this. Brigades of infantry were formed on the lines of the regular army system—four battalions—so that the Ashton and Oldham battalions which had belonged to the Manchester Brigade were attached to the two Territorial battalions of the East Lancashire Regiment although they are still known as " Manchester " battalions.

These two battalions, commanded respectively by Lieutenant-Colonel D. H. Wade and Lieutenant-Colonel J. B. Rye, left this country for service in Egypt with other units of the Division, in September 1914, and in May of the following year they went to the Dardanelles.

When the 9th Manchesters mobilised for war, the commissioned and non-commissioned ranks were only just short of the authorised establishment. The Battalion was promptly raised from a peace to a war strength, and when it moved away for Imperial Service a second and a third line were formed. Ashton has also raised a Field Artillery Brigade and a Heavy Battery. Including the townships of Stalybridge and Dukinfield, it is computed that Ashton and district have sent 14,000 men to the forces.

The Territorial Battalion spent a short period in field training in this country, and in the land of the Pharaohs they applied themselves seriously to training in the art of war. Their work in Egypt was about as strenuous as it possibly could be. For the first time the Battalion was training for war which was, for them, imminent. But exhausting as the training was in Egypt, it was not comparable to the arduous life lived on the Gallipoli Peninsula. It is impossible to exaggerate the difficulties which confronted the Ashton men and their comrades at every turn. They were fighting on an area of land which, together with the many peculiarities of the campaign, made a straightforward fight impossible. There was an absence of roads; hills that had to be negotiated were almost perpendicular; almost every movement called for disciplined heroism; dangers that could not be foreseen led to casualties, and positions which seemed to offer freedom from rifle and gun fire were invariably covered by the ubiquitous sniper. No wonder the Territorials held the view that the hottest corner of the world-war had been reserved for them.

The responsibilities of command in these circumstances could not rest lightly upon the shoulders of the officers. The student of strategy and tactics felt that his training in the art of war had been so much wasted time. Gallipoli did not offer him opportunities for strategic movements designed to place the enemy at a disadvantage. The daily order was "get cover, hold your ground, and keep a sharp look-out for any movement on the other side," for it often happened in this perplexing situation that "to be valiant is to stand"—to receive the fire of the enemy without giving way. But this plan of campaign if persisted in would suit the enemy admirably. He was defending Constantinople; the task of advancing against that place was committed to our troops.

Lieutenant Forshaw's Exploit

The Ashton men, with other East Lancashire units, shared the exacting work of holding the front-line trenches, and when the time came for assuming the offensive their courage and discipline were put to the test, for any movement outside the trenches was opposed by a hellish storm of musketry, machine-gun, and shell fire. In the early stages of the advance Second Lieutenant F. Jones was killed and Second Lieutenant J. M. Wade, son of the Commanding Officer, was reported " missing, believed killed." Lieutenant Wade was last seen jumping into a Turkish trench with his men, and inquiries made by the American Ambassador at Constantinople do not hold out any hope that he was taken prisoner. Colonel Wade was also wounded, and the officers killed include Captain Frank Hamer and Lieutenant A. E. Stringer. Major W. H. Archbutt died of wounds, and Major Hilton (Medical Officer) died in Egypt during the early training there.

The 9th Manchesters are proud of the fact that one of their number has won the Victoria Cross. On August 8, during the battle for the locality known as the vineyard, Lieutenant W. T. Forshaw with a party of his men did some very good work. " There was desperate fighting," Sir Ian Hamilton reported, " at the northern corner, where the personal bravery of Lieutenant W. T. Forshaw, who stuck to his post after his detachment had been relieved, was largely instrumental in the repulse of three very determined onslaughts." Lieutenant Forshaw has received the freedom of Ashton-under-Lyne.

Pluck and endurance have been displayed by many Ashton men. Private Robert Daley furnishes us with a noteworthy example of how a man may disregard pain if it threatens to interfere with his duty in the field. Daley was shot in the leg on June 8—about a month after landing on the Peninsula. The bullet was not deeply embedded and he extracted it himself with a knife, roughly bandaged the wound, and continued to fight. The wound, in his opinion, was too trivial to

120 9th Battalion Manchester Regiment

report to the medical authorities. A few days later he was hit with another bullet in the right arm. But he was not incapacitated, and for another two days he held his place in the firing line. Then he had the misfortune to be shot by a sniper in the eye and was this time compelled to go into hospital, where he had his right eye removed and the bullet extracted from his arm.

10TH BATTALION MANCHESTER REGIMENT
(Oldham)

THE Oldham Territorials marched to war cheerfully and with a quiet confidence in their ability to give a good account of themselves in whatever part of the field it pleased the authorities to place them.

One of the officers of the 8th Manchesters who was attached to the Oldham Battalion, writing of his experiences, said:

"I am now in a sandbag and earthen dug-out with the 10th Manchesters. I am happy to say that the continual shots and bombs and cannonade have not made me unduly nervous; in fact, I am beginning to treat them with indifference. My little dug-out is on a hill-side overlooking the Aegean sea, some 600 yards from the Turkish trenches, and continually the guns roar and re-echo over the glorious blue-green sea. We had a terrible walk with full pack along the sea-shore, over sand and stone, until we came to the ravine where the 8th Manchesters were. I found that with three exceptions every one of the officers who had joined since July had gone away sick.

"I am writing this with the Aegean Sea sparkling in the sunlight and two of our warships cruising up and down, ready to open fire. The roll of the guns of Achi Baba, just behind us, is continuous. On every yard of the earthen steps of the trenches is standing or lying a soldier, generally wrapped up in a muffler and woollen nightcap, looking something like the old pictures of a soldier in the Crimean War. The general picture is one of complete indifference to danger—though a minute does not pass without the crack of rifles and the whizz of bullets through the air and bursting bombs. Where I am is only fifteen yards from the Turkish trenches. They have put a good many bombs over, but they are nearly always caught by the so-called ' bird-cages '—large wire-netted frames standing from the parapet in a sloping position.

"You can realise the difference between this place and France. The moment you land you are under fire. The dust is dreadful, and as it is blowing half a gale it is most unpleasant; and though we were told that the fly season was over, there are still a few millions left to add to the amenities of existence. Everybody who is here in the firing line is a hero. When we see the country rising precipitously from the sea our wonder is not that we have not conquered yet, but that we have got a foothold at all."

The first big encounter with the Turco-Germanic army was on June 4, when six officers were killed and five were wounded. These casualties occurred in the bayonet charge. One of the officers who led his company in the charge describes the fighting as follows:

"June 4 was a big day for the Manchesters. After a heavy bombardment we had orders to make a bayonet charge. I had been under heavy fire before, but it was of little importance when considered in the light of what we faced on that day. I had taken three companies to reinforce the Royal Fusiliers. As Captain Gardiner and I emerged from one end of the trench a machine gun was turned on to us and a part of Gardiner's chin was shot away. However, we went down the parapet of the trench and stood on top helping the men out. When we had each assisted about three men, and the men in turn had assisted their comrades, we dashed forward to within twenty yards of the Turkish trenches. Then we lay down for a 'breather,' with musketry fire and shrapnel falling all round us. One shell burst immediately above us and poor Gardiner got eight more wounds in his back and legs. Another rush and we reached the parapet of the enemy trench. Gardiner crawled back. The trench was taken, including a German and some Turks. At this time I was accompanied by thirty-eight men. We set out with about fifty.

"I had been in the trench about ten minutes when an officer crawled in and told me that we were completely isolated, as we were the only part of that section of the line who had captured a trench up to that time. We were surrounded by Turks, but if we could hold on it would assist the remainder to get up. I said that we would hold on, and we did. When the other sections of the line got up we advanced with them and captured a few more trenches. This was on Friday afternoon. On the following day we had a comparatively quiet time. About 2.30 a.m. on Sunday morning the Turks made a terrific dash at the battalion on our left, and they had to give ground. Then our left half was forced to retire. In this retirement the commanding officer of the Royal Fusiliers was killed. I rallied my men, and after five hours' stiff fighting the trenches which we had lost were regained. The next day and night we had comparative peace, though one Turk got about 20 yards from our trench and made use of some bombs. I made a hole in him with my revolver. We had to advance a good way under rifle and machine gun fire, but it was nothing to what we had to face on the Sunday. At one time when I was standing near the trench it was a really good mix-up with Turks about five yards away. An evil-minded Turk, who from my language must have recognised me as an officer, threw a bomb at me, and a poor fellow stooping in front of me had the top of his head blown off. We were relieved the next day. Our killed and wounded included Owen, Emmott, Ascroft, Hamer Clegg, and Kirk (killed), and Nevinson, Proctor, Stott, Sutcliffe, Butterworth, and Gardiner (wounded)."

FIELD AMBULANCES

(Royal Army Medical Corps)

THE Royal Army Medical Corps was one of the branches of the service to undergo a root-and-branch reform after the South African campaign (1900-2). The system of Field Ambulances now tested in war for the first time—each ambulance is a quite independent and mobile unit—is said to have given every satisfaction in the fields of France and Flanders. But on the Gallipoli Peninsula the East Lancashire (Manchester) Field Ambulance, as an organisation, has not had a fair trial. At no time in that campaign could the divisions of the new organisation be utilised as intended. Consequently a great deal of its value from a purely administrative point of view was lost. Just the very things that must not be done "in any circumstances" were the very things that had to be done. In ordinary circumstances one would not dream of placing the clearing hospital on a shell-swept terrain. Its place would be well in rear of the firing line, in a sheltered position, and free from the distractions associated with the continuous bombardment either by our own or the enemy's guns.

But at Gallipoli all our preconceived notions as to the general conduct of a campaign had to be forgotten. Instead of the carefully planned field ambulance with its various divisions or stations separated from each other by so many hundred yards according to regulations, we had the advanced dressing station, the intermediate or

A Brave Corps 125

main dressing station, the operating tent, and clearing hospital within range of the guns. This made extremely arduous and difficult the vast responsibilities committed to the personnel of the corps.

The East Lancashire Field Ambulances are officered by some of the most highly qualified medical men in Manchester and district. When the call for Imperial Service came they (and their men) responded most nobly. They were anxious to place their surgical skill at the disposal of the country, and we now know that they have endured great hardships and privations and given of their best in one of the most difficult campaigns ever waged, and under conditions which called for an unceasing display of the military virtues of discipline and devotion to duty. Their coolness and resource, their self-sacrificing and untiring labours in tending the wounded and dying—always under fire—have won them the highest praise.

" A feature of every report, narrative, or diary I have read has been a tribute to the stretcher-bearers," writes General Sir Ian Hamilton, in one of his dispatches. " All ranks, from Generals in Command to wounded men in hospital, are unanimous in their praise. I have watched a party from the moment when the telephone summoned them from their dug-out to the time when they returned with their wounded. To see them run light-heartedly across the fire-swept slopes is to be privileged to witness a superb example of the hero in man. No braver corps exists, and I believe the reason to be that all thought of self is instinctively flung aside when the saving of others is the motive."

As soon as the Medical Corps set foot on the Peninsula they found a large number of wounded waiting for treatment. The casualty clearing station was filled with them, and there were no hospital ships to take them off. It was imperative that they should be removed without delay, and empty transports were pressed into the service. B Section of No. 2 Field Ambulance joined one of these temporary hospital ships, which was crowded with wounded for Alexandria. The boat could not be properly staffed, so that it was only possible to attend to the wounded in a very ordinary way. Bandages and dressing unfortunately ran short, and some of the men had to be neglected until Alexandria was reached. Sections of other Field Ambulances also staffed hospital ships, and officers were detached for duty on drifters, etc.

The end of the Peninsula was dominated by the Turkish fire, and it was practically impossible to find a safe place to pitch tents. The only alternative was to get underground. The 3rd Field Ambulance, commanded by Lieutenant-Colonel W. M. Steinthal, dug themselves in and hoisted the Red Cross flag, which the Turks respected. Sometimes a stray shot would cause anxiety, but there was no deliberate attempt on the part of the enemy to fire on the non-combatant service. The 1st Field Ambulance, commanded by Lieutenant-Colonel H. G. Parker, entrenched themselves on the cliff opposite Imbros. This proved to be a good and safe site as the shells from the Asiatic side either dropped short or fell into the sea.

The fighting area was so limited that it was not possible to get far away from combatants. One hundred yards in the rear was a field bakery, and about 150 yards away were two 60-pounders. The Turks paid some attention to these guns daily, and several men of the Medical Service were killed by shells that fell short. Dressing stations were established near the firing line, and intermediate dressing stations were set up midway between the fire trenches and the main bivouac. After some hard digging a fairly safe place for an operating tent was hacked out of the cliff side. This tent was manned by the 1st Field Ambulance and the officer in charge was Captain J. Morley, the Manchester surgeon, who did great service under very adverse circumstances. Casualties were passing through the dressing stations in large numbers daily.

In the big engagement on June 4, when the Manchesters

Buried at Sea

suffered so heavily, the Field Ambulances dealt with over two thousand cases. The officers and men of the Medical Service on this and subsequent days performed many acts of gallantry in attending to patients. Several of their number were killed and two officers wounded. On June 10 Lieutenant-Colonel W. B. Pritchard, the Commanding Officer of the 2nd Field Ambulance, landed on the Peninsula, having previously been engaged at Alexandria and Mudros. There was at this time a lull in the fighting, and the Field Ambulances took advantage of this opportunity to improve their dressing stations and bivouac. They also prepared safe places for the wounded when waiting for their removal to a hospital ship. The dressing stations were in the middle of what was known as Shrapnel Valley, and it was in the neighbourhood of these that most of the Medical Corps casualties occurred. These dressing stations were about two miles from the cliffs, and it was a very hazardous business visiting them, as one never knew when the Turks might decide to cover the ground with high explosive or shrapnel. Saps and mule tracks had not yet been cut, and troops moving about were easily " spotted." On June 23 the 2nd Field Ambulance relieved the 1st Field Ambulance in the dressing stations, and it was on this day that Captain F. C. Bentz was badly injured at the intermediate dressing station. The Turkish batteries had opened fire upon a body of men moving near this station, and Captain Bentz when dressing a wounded man was hit in the back with a piece of shrapnel. He was removed to hospital and later to a hospital ship, where he made a remarkable recovery. Captain Bentz is now doing light duty in this country.

On the following day Colonel Pritchard, the Commander of the Ambulance, was mortally wounded. Colonel Pritchard was inspecting the dressing stations. He had passed through the main dressing station, which was commanded by his brother, Major H. W. Pritchard, and promising to be back at 4 p.m. he proceeded to the advanced dressing stations. About 3.30 p.m. the Lancashire Fusiliers relieved the Manchesters in the fire trenches and many men were passing up and down in the open. Suddenly the Turks opened fire with shrapnel and there were many casualties, including Colonel Pritchard, who was severely wounded in the head. When in the operating tent he recognised his brother and inquired of him if he had many wounded to attend to, at the same time noticing that wounded men were being brought in from the field. Almost his last words were: " I'm all right ; attend to those patients." He was removed to the operating tent about two miles away, where Captain Morley removed a shrapnel bullet which had fractured the skull. Later Colonel Pritchard was removed to the hospital ship *Somali*. He died on June 29 (1915) and was buried at sea near Malta.

For the big battle early in August the Medical Corps had to erect more dressing stations within easy reach of the fire trenches. How were such dressing stations formed? The ground was carefully reconnoitred, and when the best positions were agreed upon a working party began to " dig in." The site chosen for the August battle was a slight depression on the left of a dry watercourse. This watercourse zigzagged down from the foot of Achi Baba and made a natural trench which was continued by a mule track and was chiefly used for rationing troops in the front trenches. It was also used as a sheltered way to and from the trenches. Its walls would average about 7 feet high, so that the men and mules were protected from direct rifle and shell fire. The dressing station was to be ready by the evening of August 6. Protected by the walls of the ravine, the men dug out a roomy compartment about 20 feet long and 14 feet wide with walls 8 feet high. An abutment of sandbags was built to intercept enfilading rifle fire. The bullets were nearly spent when they reached this spot, but very nasty

At the Dressing Station

wounds were occasionally caused by them. During the day the Assistant Director of Medical Services sent word that the station must be ready on the 5th, and in order to comply with this request the men were continually digging in relays until dusk, when the station was ready for its equipment. The attack was intended as a surprise for the enemy, so that all the material was quietly carried from the base along the mule track on stretchers, a distance of about two and a half miles. This was no light task in the blazing August sun. By 10 a.m. on the 5th the dressing station was complete and the men were " told off " to their respective duties as bearers, ward nurses, cooks, water-men, etc.

The action was to begin promptly at 9 a.m. on the next day by a heavy bombardment of the enemy's position by guns of the fleet as well as the guns on land. But the Turks anticipated us. They seemed to have got news of our operations and they commenced the battle about fifteen minutes before our bombardment was timed to begin. For two hours the roar of the guns was deafening and shells were dropping all round the dressing station. Some damage was caused by splinters. When the infantry advance took place the Red Cross flag was hoisted over the position. It was not long before the medical officers and dressers were busy with casualties. There was a never-ending procession of bearers carrying the dead, wounded, and dying. The men were lying on all sides. The medical officers inspected the tallies upon which the regimental medical officers had described the injuries so that the most seriously wounded might receive early attention. Rifles, accoutrements, and blood-stained uniform lie about in all directions.

But the dressing station is only a halting-place. As the cases were dressed those who could walk took shelter in dug-outs until the fire had died down, when an officer piloted them to the ambulance wagons. To reach these wagons an open stretch of terrain had to be crossed which was continually swept by spent bullets from the enemy's firing line, and several of the bearers were hit. The most difficult part of the work was in getting the lying-down cases to the wagons.

The bearers did their work fearlessly. In the first hour about one hundred cases passed through the station. Later, as the attack was not pressed home, the number of casualties considerably decreased, and by nightfall all the cases had been dealt with and sent down to the clearing hospital at the base. It is really astonishing how well the wounded behaved throughout the campaign. There was a good supply of cigarettes, and these seemed to console them more than the morphia needle which was used in the bad cases. Three or four men came down to the station suffering from shell shock caused by a shell that had burst among them. How they escaped death, much less serious injury, is a miracle. One of these men had taken part in the original landing with the "incomparable 29th" and each succeeding engagement. He said that when the shell burst he thought the end of the world had come.

Except for some desultory firing the fight was practically over when darkness came on. The Turks made a counter-attack later, but did not make any headway, and our casualties were few. In the absence of orders to move forward it was concluded that the attack higher up on the Peninsula had not succeeded. Gradually the news of the failure at Suvla Bay filtered through, and was very disheartening to the troops, as they had confidently looked forward to success after all the hard fighting and the sacrifices made. The dressing stations were now taken over by the Field Ambulances of the 52nd Division, and the East Lancashires returned to their headquarters on the cliff, where many of the men had to be treated for jaundice, dysentery, and septic sores. The casualties in the Medical Corps were heavy. In the 2nd Field Ambulance the Commanding Officer died from wounds, another

Casualties among "Medicals"

officer was badly wounded, and about twelve of the rank and file were killed and about sixty wounded. The other two Ambulances suffered proportionately, although these units were fortunate in not having an officer killed.

There have been many details of administration which seem to call for criticism. But it is possible that when the whole truth is known it may be found that criticism which might be offered at this period would have to be readjusted and perhaps rejected altogether. Circumstances are sometimes stronger than organisation. Our plans may be well devised; practically every likely contingency may have been provided for. But neither the best-laid schemes nor the most perfect organisation could be expected to meet the varying conditions of service in Gallipoli.

GREAT BUT UNAVAILING GALLANTRY: WHY?

THE campaign on the Gallipoli Peninsula might be described as a Pyrrhic victory. But the valour of our brave soldiers, whose constancy and courage under fearful odds transcended even Spartan achievement, made it glorious and memorable. It was from first to last a great adventure. The success of our arms in that field would have been attended with momentous results in other fields, and if we had failed to take Constantinople—had simply "held" the Turks before Achi Baba—the gain to us would have been worth the sacrifice it involved.

Since the evacuation of the Peninsula, criticism, for the most part hostile and generally ill-informed, has been circulated. When our expectations have not been realised—expectations often based upon unreliable information—as was the case at Gallipoli and Kut-el-Amara, our soldiers have had to submit to an excessively cold douche of criticism unrelentingly poured upon them by men seemingly indifferent to those claims which go to the making of intelligent and helpful criticism. Any passing rumour having its source in the wildest imagination has been grasped and bruited about for the purpose of discrediting those who are bearing the heat and burden of the day.

Why did we fail? In some quarters our failure has been attributed to the employment of so many non-regular troops (the 29th Division was the only Division of Regular British troops on the Peninsula). We have

Territorials' Fighting Qualities 133

yet to learn that General Sir Ian Hamilton has the shadow of a complaint to make against any of his troops. On the contrary, his dispatches go to prove that he was full of admiration for their unexampled valour. The East Lancashire Territorials, from the beginning of their fighting to the end of it, did just as well as their comrades of the Line, for they were animated by the strong moral cement of Lancashire *esprit de county*. They knew that the people of Lancashire were following their every movement, closely watching their conduct, their soldierly bearing, and their discipline; that they were intensely eager to learn about their fighting qualities and their courage, their self-control in the hour of victory, the strength of their moral fibre in the hour of adversity. From the point of view of cohesion and tradition the Division had nothing to learn. This gave them the valuable quality of self-confidence—a quality which was further increased when they found in General Sir Ian Hamilton a commander who trusted them and employed them exactly as he would any Regular Division. The quotations I have given from Sir Ian Hamilton's dispatches show conclusively that his troops *never failed* him.

But their courage and the courage of the other troops failed to produce victorious results in so far as they were never able to accomplish the specific task set them; never able to clear the Narrows for the Fleet. The Lancashires may have helped to save Egypt from invasion and to have killed or wounded 200,000 Turks, but they did not clear the Narrows. Why? Was it the fault of the officers and men? Obviously not. Was it the fault of the plan of operations or of the handling of the troops generally? I believe when the official papers are made public the country will be satisfied that the fault did not rest here. If, then, neither the Commander-in-Chief nor the troops are to be blamed, where does the responsibility for our failure rest?

Our failure, I submit, does not rest with the Com-

134 Great but Unavailing Gallantry: Why?

mander-in-Chief nor with his troops—Regular or Territorial—who so resplendently opened the campaign. But any promise of victory gradually faded away as the months lengthened, because satisfactory reinforcements were not hurried to the scene after the early and heavy fighting. War has never been successfully waged when the wastage incident to war has been ignored. Imagine the position of a commander who is faced with a continual decline in his military strength whilst at the same time the attainment of his object demands even greater exertions than have yet been made! The daily toll of casualties ran into hundreds and there were no drafts to fill up the gaps. The East Lancashire and other Divisions were allowed to exhaust their strength in brilliant onslaughts against Achi Baba until the time came when the hospitals accounted for more men than the firing line. No restorative in the form of efficient drafts was supplied, and when the evacuation took place each of the Divisions was reduced to a skeleton. Did the authorities imagine that, phœnix-like, those who had fallen would rise again to take their places in the ranks?

There is no more detestable heresy in military matters than to let veteran formations die away and to think to make good the deficit by throwing into the field new and comparatively raw formations. This heresy is hundreds of years old. In the American Civil war a Wisconsin Regiment was known to be worth three other regiments. The reason was that that State used its recruits for keeping its old formations up to strength. The amalgam of veterans and keen fresh youngsters was marvellous. The other States let their old battalions dwindle away to nothing and then brought up new battalions composed of men without war experience, and they soon melted away in the fight.

What happened at Gallipoli? The men of the old battalions, seeing themselves dwindling away from 1,000 to 500, then to 400, next to 250, and in some cases to

100, lost hope and became sore distressed. The new formations had not the necessary stiffening of old soldiers with them to give them confidence, and had not half the value—not one-third of the value—of troops poured in to fill an old cadre. Let me put it in another way : If instead of three new Divisions for Suvla Bay, the General Officer Commanding had had one new Division and the other two had been used to supply drafts to keep up to strength the East Lancashires, and the Lowland and Naval Divisions, the number of Divisions at the Commander's disposal would have looked less formidable on paper, but actually the fighting value of the force would have been twice what it was.

Lastly, we failed because the starving policy did not stop at trained men. Munitions were scarce, and especially high-explosive shell. Victory in these conditions was impossible. Our troops did well to " hold " the Turks for so many months. When we ceased from troubling them they were free for other fields, and General Townshend and his gallant men fell into their hands.

The strength of the British has always lain in their tenacity; their weakness in want of imagination. Had the supreme direction in London been able to realise that the moral force animating our Lancashire lads at Cape Helles was actually thriving upon danger, difficulty, and resistance, they might then have found strength to harden their own hearts. To the fighting troops, as to their Chief, evacuation had, by degrees, become unthinkable. At home, by degrees, the foe had become more and more formidable until, at last, evacuation set the definite seal of failure upon the most gallant adventure in history.

EAST LANCASHIRE TERRITORIAL DIVISION

Honours and Rewards

OFFICERS and men of the East Lancashire Territorials by their gallantry and devotion to duty in the Gallipoli campaign have gained many honours and rewards. Unfortunately many gallant deeds have not been officially recognised because of a lack of witnesses due to heavy casualties among the officers.

Every effort has been made to make this list complete, but the compiler cannot claim to have succeeded. The difficulties encountered in preparing any list makes one feel that it does not possess the merit of completeness.

DIVISIONAL STAFF

Major-General WILLIAM DOUGLAS, C.B., D.S.O., General Officer Commanding the 42nd (East Lancashire) Division—K.C.M.G.

Major (temporary Lieutenant-Colonel) ARTHUR WYNDHAM TUFNELL, Royal West Surrey Regiment, Staff Officer to Major-General Sir William Douglas, now Brigadier-General, East Lancashire Infantry Brigade—C.M.G. and promoted to Brevet Lieutenant-Colonel for distinguished service in the field.

Major L. W. LA T. COCKCRAFT, R.A., formerly staff officer to Brigadier-General A. D'A. King—appointed D.A.A.G.

Mentioned in Dispatches—Major R. S. ALLEN, Hampshire Regiment, Deputy Assistant Adjutant and Quartermaster-General.

BRIGADE COMMANDERS

Mentioned in Dispatches—Colonel H. C. FRITH (temporary Brigadier-General) Commanding Lancashire Fusiliers Brigade;

Honours and Rewards

Colonel NOEL LEE (temporary Brigadier-General) Commanding Manchester Infantry Brigade, Hon. Colonel 6th Battalion Manchester Regiment (died of wounds).

THE BLACKBURN ARTILLERY

Lieutenant-Colonel ARTHUR BIRTWISTLE, Brigade Commander—C.M.G.

Major JOHN COWAN BROWNING, Commander of the 5th Lancashire (Church) Battery—D.S.O.

Sergeant J. D. FITZPATRICK, 5th Lancashire Battery—D.C.M.

Sergeant J. BRADSHAW, 5th Lancashire Battery—D.C.M.

Battery Quartermaster-Sergeant S. W. H. GASTALL, 5th Lancashire Battery—D.C.M.

Sergeant C. TAYLOR, 5th Lancashire Battery—D.C.M.

Sergeant W. C. SUNDERLAND, 6th Lancashire Battery—D.C.M.

Gunner S. VARLEY, 5th Lancashire Battery—D.C.M.

Gunner H. DAWSON, 5th Lancashire Battery—D.C.M.

Gunner H. OGDEN, Ammunition Column—D.C.M.

Driver J. WILSON, 5th Lancashire Battery—D.C.M.

Mentioned in Dispatches—Lieutenant-Colonel A. BIRTWISTLE; Major J. C. BROWNING; Sergeant J. D. FITZPATRICK; Gunner S. VARLEY; Gunner J. R. WILSON.

THE BOLTON ARTILLERY

Corporal J. G. JONES, 19th Lancashire Battery—D.C.M.

For conspicuous gallantry. After being wounded he kept up a steady rate of fire with his gun, and displayed great coolness and courage.

Corporal T. GRIME, Ammunition Column, 18th Lancashire Battery—Médaille Militaire.

ROYAL ENGINEERS (FIELD AND SIGNAL COMPANIES)

Lieutenant-Colonel S. L. TENNANT—Croix de Guerre.

Lieutenant OSCAR TAUNTON (died of wounds)—Military Cross.

For conspicuous gallantry on June 4, 1915, during operations south of Krithia, Dardanelles, when he held back the enemy from advancing along a trench on the left flank which was much exposed. By means of bombs and hand grenades he personally held his position for over two hours. He picked up several of the enemy's bombs and threw them back before they exploded.

Captain G. W. DENISON (Adjutant)—Promoted to Major.

Lieutenant (now Captain) GORDON LESLIE BROAD—Military Cross.

Second Lieutenant W. ALLARD—Croix de Guerre.

Company Quarter-master Sergeant WILLIAMS, Signal Company—D.C.M.

For laying lines under fire prior to big attack on June 4, 1915.

Sergeant-Instructor F. J. SOWRAY—Croix de Guerre.

Sapper A. JONES—D.C.M.

Sapper A. BRODERICK (died of wounds)—D.C.M.

For gallantry displayed in repairing communication lines under fire.

Sapper A. GOURLAY—D.C.M.

For conspicuous gallantry and devotion to duty. He has been twice wounded.

Sergeant (Acting Company S.M.) A. NEEDHAM—D.C.M.

For consistent gallantry and devotion to duty. He has distinguished himself in daring night work, and has set a fine example.

Signaller E. H. VICK, Signal Company—D.C.M.

For conspicuous gallantry whilst repairing telephones under heavy fire.

Mentioned in Dispatches—Lieutenant-Colonel S. L. TENNANT; Major L. F. WELLS, A.M.Inst.C.E.; Lieutenant (now Captain G. L. BROAD; Second Lieutenant R. B. ANGUS (killed); Sergeant W. WATTERS; Lance-Corporal T. G. HALSALL; Lance-Corporal F. RHODES; Sapper B. BARLOW; Sapper T. HINSLEY; Sapper W. KNOTT; Sapper H. SMITH.

5TH BATTALION LANCASHIRE FUSILIERS

Lieutenant-Colonel JAMES ISHERWOOD—C.B.

Major GEORGE BENSON GLEN WOOD (Adjutant)—D.S.O.

Captain WALTER HORRIDGE—Military Cross.

Honours and Rewards

Lieutenant ROBERT WHITTAKER BUTCHER—Military Cross.

Colour-Sergeant (acting Sergeant-Major) J. ROBINSON—Médaille Militaire.

Lance-Corporal WILD—D.C.M.

Lance-Corporal J. NEWSHAM—D.C.M.

    For consistent devotion to duty as a stretcher-bearer. He twice left his trench in full view of the enemy to attend to wounded men in the wire.

Mentioned in Dispatches—Lieutenant-Colonel J. ISHERWOOD; Major G. B. G. WOOD; Hon. Major and Quartermaster J. CREMAN; Captain E. ASHWORTH; Captain W. HORRIDGE; Lieutenant R. W. BUTCHER; Private A. BENTLEY; Private H. BERRY.

6TH BATTALION LANCASHIRE FUSILIERS

Major R. L. LEES—D.S.O.

Captain EDWARD WOOLMER—Military Cross.

Second Lieutenant (temporary Captain) ROBERT PHIPPS HORNBY—Military Cross.

Sergeant-Major B. ALLISTER—D.C.M.

    For the good leading of his platoon south of Krithia (Dardanelles) on June 4 under heavy rifle and shrapnel fire to take a Turkish trench. The report recommending him for reward states that he cleared one flank himself, killing eight Turks.

Private J. CRYER—D.C.M.

Private J. W. CHILD—D.C.M.

    For gallant conduct on June 4, 1915, south-west of Krithia (Dardanelles) in volunteering to attack a redoubt and holding it with four other men until relieved ten hours later. He had previously been mentioned for gallant conduct.

Mentioned in Dispatches—Major R. L. LEES; Captain A. L. SPAFFORD (Adjutant—killed); Captain E. WOOLMER; Second Lieutenant (temporary Captain) R. P. HORNBY; Private J. DOUGHTY; Private E. HARTLEY.

7TH BATTALION LANCASHIRE FUSILIERS

Major (temporary Lieutenant-Colonel) W. J. LAW (killed)—Croix de Guerre.

Major C. T. ALEXANDER—D.S.O.

Captain (temporary Major) REGINALD P. W. GLEDHILL, Royal Irish Regiment (Adjutant)—Military Cross.

Captain C. C. FITZGERALD, Royal Army Medical Corps (attached)—Military Cross.

Lieutenant MORRISON (attached)—Military Cross.

Second Lieutenant (temporary Captain) A. W. BOYD—Military Cross.

For conspicuous gallantry. He was appointed to command an attack after his Commanding Officer had been killed, and carried it through with success, displaying great boldness and determination as a leader. When the enemy had recaptured a crater by a counter-attack he at once placed himself at the head of a party of grenadiers and drove them out. (This was one of the bravest acts in the Gallipoli campaign. The crater was officially named " Boyd's crater.")

Corporal W. DOWNTON—D.C.M.

For gallantry and devotion on June 4, during an action south of Krithia. Under an officer and one other man Downton charged and captured a small Turkish redoubt and continued to hold it after the officer was killed, using Turkish rifles and ammunition when their own was exhausted. On August 7 he was wounded in two places, but recovered and returned to the trenches. On December 19 he volunteered to accompany Captain Boyd when the mine head was destroyed. For his service on this occasion he was awarded a bar to his D.C.M. He was killed shortly afterwards.

Sergeant T. FIELD—D.C.M.

Corporal J. BLACKLOCK—D.C.M.

Private F. MOTTERSHEAD—D.C.M.

For conspicuous gallantry in volunteering to destroy the entrance to one of the enemy's mine shafts. He carried a bag

Honours and Rewards

of explosive round his neck and placed it in position actually within the enemy's trench. He then returned over the wire entanglements laying the electric connection. It was later discovered that the entrance had been completely destroyed by the explosion.

Private CASEY—D.C.M.

For gallantry on May 10 when the Battalion moved to take up a new position in the firing line. Private Casey showed great bravery in the face of heavy fire from the enemy trenches.

Private W. PRINCE—D.C.M.

For gallant conduct on June 5, south-west of Krithia, in charging and capturing a small redoubt, accompanied by two men and an officer. Although the officer was killed, the small party held the redoubt, using Turkish rifles and ammunition when their own was finished, until reinforced.

Sergeant A. HARVEY—D.C.M.

For conspicuous gallantry. When his machine-gun team had lost two men during a bombardment, he withdrew to another position and reopened fire, although the gun had been damaged.

Private C. BENT—D.C.M.

For conspicuous gallantry during the occupation of a crater made by a mine explosion and during a counter-attack carried out later.

Mentioned in Dispatches—Major (temporary Lieutenant-Colonel) W. J. LAW (killed); Captain M. R. P. W. GLEDHILL; Lieutenant BENNETT BURLEIGH (died of wounds); Sergeant T. FIELD; Corporal J. BLACKLOCK; Corporal R. GINDER; Lance-Corporal E. J. HOPKINS; Private B. V. BISHOP (killed); Private J. CLARKE; Private D. GRESTY.

8TH BATTALION LANCASHIRE FUSILIERS

Major (now temporary Lieutenant-Colonel) HAROLD ALEC KIRKBY (Adjutant)—D.S.O.

Second Lieutenant (temporary Lieutenant) REGINALD ALDERSON —Military Cross.

He performed a gallant act on the night of August 8 by leaving the section of his trench in order to throw a bomb into

142 East Lancashire Territorial Division

the section of the same trench which was at that time occupied by the Turks. He was slightly wounded.

Private A. FARNWORTH—D.C.M.

Farnworth was not quite eighteen when he received the D.C.M. for his gallantry during the fighting near Krithia on June 6 when he on four occasions brought in wounded under fire. In the following month this gallant young soldier died from wounds received in the neighbourhood of the bivouac.

Mentioned in Dispatches—Lieutenant-Colonel J. A. FALLOWS (killed); Major H. A. KIRKBY (Adjutant); Captain A. J. GOODFELLOW (died of wounds); Lance-Corporal W. HODGES; Private F. T. ABRAHAM; Private G. WOOD.

5TH BATTALION MANCHESTER REGIMENT

Lieutenant-Colonel H. C. DARLINGTON—C.M.G.

Captain JOHN MALCOLM BRODIE SANDARS, Leinster Regiment (Adjutant)—Military Cross.

Second Lieutenant MILES KENNETH BURROWS—Military Cross.

Sergeant G. BLYTH—D.C.M.

For conspicuous gallantry on several occasions, notably when in charge of a body of snipers he fearlessly exposed himself in order to set an example at a critical moment.

Sergeant C. BARNES—D.C.M.

For conspicuous good work during operations; also during heavy bombardments by the enemy.

Company Sergeant-Major T. McCARTY—D.C.M.

For consistent gallantry and good work under heavy fire.

Acting Sergeant-Major J. MORRISON—D.C.M.

For consistent gallantry and good work. He set a fine example when replenishing ammunition and bomb stores under heavy fire.

Private T. SEDDON—D.C.M.

For conspicuous gallantry as a stretcher-bearer. He lost his leg by shell fire when rushing to assist a wounded man, although he was himself wounded at the time.

Honours and Rewards

Private R. BENT—D.C.M.

Private R. W. WARD—D.C.M.

Corporal J. McCARTNEY—D.C.M.

Private A. DAVIES—D.C.M.

Private A. HILTON—D.C.M.

Private S. STOCKTON—D.C.M.

Private J. GRIMES—Croix de Guerre.

Mentioned in Dispatches—Lieutenant-Colonel H. C. DARLINGTON; Captain J. M. B. SANDARS; Captain W. T. WOODS; Lieutenant G. S. JAMES (killed); Lieutenant P. C. CLAYTON; Second Lieutenant M. K. BURROWS; Sergeant W. S. WHITTLE (killed); Lance-Corporal F. CATTERALL; Private R. W. WARD; Private R. BENT.

6TH BATTALION MANCHESTER REGIMENT

Major (temporary Lieutenant-Colonel) CHARLES RAYMOND PILKINGTON—C.M.G.

Major CHARLES SWANWICK WORTHINGTON—D.S.O.

Captain P. V. HOLBERTON (Adjutant)—Promoted to Brevet Major and General Staff Officer (2nd grade).

Second Lieutenant (temporary Lieutenant) SIDNEY COLLIER—Military Cross.

Corporal (now Second Lieutenant) E. P. HARTSHORN—D.C.M.

Company Sergeant-Major (now Lieutenant) HAY—D.C.M.

During the operations of June 4, at Krithia, Sergeant-Major Hay, consequent upon casualties to officers, was left in command of his company and held the advanced line till compelled to fall back owing to flank retirement. Though wounded twice in the arm and sustaining another slight wound, he brought his company back in good order.

Company Sergeant-Major HURDLEY—D.C.M.

Lance-Corporal W. A. SENIOR—D.C.M.
For conspicuous gallantry on June 4 during operations in the Gallipoli Peninsula. He showed great bravery, coolness, and resource in leading a party from traverse to traverse, which resulted in the capture of a Turkish officer and about sixty other prisoners.

Private McLAREN DOIG—D.C.M.
For an act of bravery in Gallipoli Peninsula on June 4 during the famous charge of the Manchesters. In this engagement Doig was wounded, and after six weeks in hospital at Alexandria he returned to the firing line and was mortally wounded on August 11.

Private J. MURPHY—D.C.M.

Private R. HASHIM—D.C.M.

Private G. R. CUTTER—D.C.M.

Lance-Sergeant A. McDONALD—D.C.M.
For conspicuous gallantry on August 7, 1915, at Gallipoli. Twice he crossed a very dangerous fire-swept zone to bring up bombs to the firing line. On the third occasion he found a wounded officer whom he brought in.

Sergeant R. W. GILL—D.C.M.
For conspicuous good work with machine guns on several occasions. Despite his fifty-six years, he had done great execution among the enemy.

Company Sergeant-Major A. McDOWELL—D.C.M. and Médaille Militaire.
For conspicuous gallantry. When his company officers had become casualties he rallied his company under heavy fire and led them to the attack.

Mentioned in Dispatches—Major (temporary Lieutenant-Colonel) C. R. PILKINGTON ; Major C. S. WORTHINGTON ; Captain (now Major) P. V. HOLBERTON (twice) ; Captain H. B. PILKINGTON (killed) ; Lieutenant (temporary Captain) H. A. HAMMICK ; Company Sergeant-Major HAY ; Company Sergeant-Major J. HURDLEY ; Lance-Sergeant B. C. CORY ; Lance-Corporal W. A. SENIOR ; Private A. B. (now Corporal) A. B. SMITH ; Private N. T. WILLS ; Private A. M. DOIG ; Private R. CUTTER ; Private R. HASHIM.

Honours and Rewards

7TH BATTALION MANCHESTER REGIMENT

Captain (temporary Major) ARTHUR EDWARD FLYNN FAWCUS—Military Cross and Croix de Guerre.

Major Fawcus took a distinguished part in the battle of Achi Baba on June 4, and for his cool leading and the initiative he displayed, and for the fine example he set his men in a desperate situation, he received the British and the French decorations.

Captain PETER HUBERT CREAGH (Leicestershire Regiment), Adjutant—D.S.O.

For his conduct of the operations after Major Staveacre fell.

Captain G. CHADWICK—Military Cross.

Captain Chadwick and his little band of men displayed great gallantry in the action on August 6–7. The men had to advance out of a narrow nullah upon which Turkish machine guns were trained. They lost heavily, both in killed and wounded. Captain Chadwick by his example and daring encouraged his men to hold on and helped to save a situation which was becoming extremely dangerous for other units of the battalion.

Captain NORMAN H. P. WHITLEY—Military Cross.

Captain Whitley saved the life of a wounded soldier by crawling two hundred yards under heavy fire at Cape Helles with the man on his back.

Captain J. F. FARROW (Medical Officer)—Military Cross.

For gallantry in attending wounded throughout the campaign in Gallipoli.

Captain J. N. BROWN—Promoted to Brevet Major.

Rev. G. T. KERBY (Chaplain)—Military Cross.

Private M. RICHARDSON—D.C.M.

For conspicuous gallantry on June 4 and 5 during operations near Krithia in holding alone a trench against the enemy who were in the same trench, and continuing to keep them at bay until wounded on the evening of the 5th. By his tenacity this portion of the trench remained in our hands.

Private (now Corporal) F. WHITE—D.C.M.

In the battle of August 6 Private White of C Company was one of a small party who advanced under a heavy fire against the enemy. He remained under cover firing at the enemy until late in the day, when he crawled back to a place of safety. Most of the men who were with him were shot down.

Company Sergeant-Major W. MORT—D.C.M.

For consistent and conspicuous gallantry throughout the operations on the Gallipoli Peninsula. He invariably set a fine example of devotion to duty and disregard of danger.

Company Sergeant-Major T. OGDEN—D.C.M.

Mentioned in Dispatches—Major J. H. STAVEACRE (killed); Captain P. H. CREAGH (Adjutant); Lance-Corporal H. S. MCCARTNEY; Lance-Corporal J. FRANK; Private J. CONNOLLY.

8TH BATTALION MANCHESTER REGIMENT

Captain A. E. BARLOW—Military Cross.

Corporal (now Sergeant) W. M. MCLAUGHTON—D.C.M.

Lance-Corporal W. STANTON—D.C.M.

For gallant conduct on June 4, south of Krithia. He advanced across the open under heavy fire with a rope to one of the enemy's abandoned machine guns, which was by this means dragged in and captured.

Private J. O'CONNOR—D.C.M.

For bringing up ammunition during the attack on June 4–5 under heavy rifle and shrapnel fire, and for carrying wounded comrades to a place of safety. O'Connor was twice wounded.

Company Sergeant-Major BRENNAN—D.C.M.

For conspicuous gallantry when establishing a post within a few yards of an occupied enemy trench. He refused to leave the post for thirty-six hours till the work was finished.

Lance-Corporal A. COLLENS—D.C.M.

For conspicuous devotion to duty. He worked for seven hours in the construction of a trench under a sustained rifle fire.

Honours and Rewards

Corporal E. TWIGG—D.C.M.
For conspicuous gallantry when working on a trench for several hours under sustained rifle fire.

Mentioned in Dispatches—Lieutenant-Colonel W. G. HEYS (killed); Captain E. G. W. OLDFIELD (killed); Captain H. J. ROSE (killed); Captain D. H. STANDRING (died of wounds); Captain H. C. LINGS; Sergeant-Major P. MURPHY (attached); Company Sergeant-Major E. GARSIDE (killed); Corporal J. WILLIAMS; Private G. EVANS.

9TH BATTALION MANCHESTER REGIMENT

Lieutenant WILLIAM THOMAS FORSHAW—V.C.
For most conspicuous bravery and determination in the Gallipoli Peninsula from August 7 to 9, 1915. When holding the north-west corner of the Vineyard he was attacked and heavily bombed by Turks, who advanced time after time by three trenches which converged at this point. But he held his own, not only directing his men and encouraging them by exposing himself with the utmost disregard to danger, but personally throwing bombs continuously for forty-nine hours. When his detachment was relieved after twenty-four hours he volunteered to continue the direction of operations.

Three times during the night of August 8–9 he was again heavily attacked, and once the Turks were over the barricade. But after shooting three with his revolver he led his men forward and recaptured it. When he rejoined his battalion he was choked and sickened by bomb fumes, badly bruised by fragments of shrapnel, and could barely lift his arm from the continuous bomb throwing. It was due to his personal example, magnificent courage, and endurance that this very important corner was held.

Lieutenant-Colonel D. H. WADE—Promoted to temporary rank of Brigadier-General.

Major and Quartermaster M. H. CONNERY—Military Cross.
For services throughout Gallipoli campaign.

Lieutenant ROBERT GARSIDE WOOD — The Military Cross and Croix de Guerre.

148 East Lancashire Territorial Division

Second Lieutenant CHARLES EARSHAM COOKE—Military Cross.

Second Lieutenant (temporary Captain) OLIVER JEPSON SUTTON —Military Cross.

Lance-Corporal A. DAVIS—D.C.M.

For conspicuous gallantry when covering a retirement under a very heavy fire at a few yards range.

Private S. LITTLEFORD—D.C.M.

For conspicuous gallantry in flinging a lighted bomb over the parapet, and thus probably saving many casualties. He was himself wounded in the arm by the explosion.

Sergeant J. GREENHALGH—D.C.M.

For conspicuous gallantry when covering a retirement under heavy fire at a few yards range.

Lance-Corporal S. PEARSON—D.C.M.

Corporal T. PICKFORD—D.C.M.

Private F. CHEVALIER—D.C.M.

Sergeant S. BAYLEY—D.C.M.

Sergeant GRANTHAM—D.C.M.

Corporal SILVESTER—D.C.M.

Mentioned in Dispatches—Lieutenant R. G. WOOD; Second Lieutenant (temporary Lieutenant) O. J. SUTTON; Private W. BURKE (died of wounds); Private J. E. TAYLOR; Private T. WESTON; Private G. A. SMITH.

10TH BATTALION MANCHESTER REGIMENT

Second Lieutenant (temporary Lieutenant) HANDEL HASSALL— Military Cross.

Corporal F. BADDELEY—D.C.M.

For conspicuous gallantry on several occasions when in charge of a grenadier party. He also made a very gallant reconnaissance alone, entering the enemy's trench and bringing back valuable information.

4TH BATTALION EAST LANCASHIRE REGIMENT

Lieutenant Arthur John Dixon Robinson—Military Cross.

Private T. Smith—D.C.M.

For conspicuous gallantry. He went out on his own initiative in broad daylight to attempt the rescue of a wounded man who was lying within 80 yards of the enemy's lines. He was wounded in three places, and forced to crawl back.

Mentioned in Dispatches—Captain and Hon. Major E. L. Carus; Lieutenant A. J. D. Robinson; Second Lieutenant A. F. Behrend; Private J. L. Cooke; Acting Corporal J. Hargreaves.

5TH BATTALION EAST LANCASHIRE REGIMENT

Second Lieutenant Alfred Victor Smith—V.C. and Croix de Guerre.

For most conspicuous bravery. He was in the act of throwing a grenade when it slipped from his hand and fell to the bottom of the trench close to several of our officers and men. He immediately shouted a warning, and himself jumped clear and into safety, but seeing that the officers and men were unable to get cover, and knowing well that the grenade was due to explode, he returned without any hesitation and flung himself down on it. He was instantly killed by the explosion. His magnificent act of self-sacrifice undoubtedly saved many lives.

Lance-Corporal G. Whitehead—D.C.M.

For conspicuous gallantry when in charge of scouts. He carried messages repeatedly under very heavy fire.

Bandsman Cook—D.C.M.

ARMY SERVICE CORPS (TRANSPORT AND SUPPLY COLUMN)

Major Reginald Joseph Slaughter (Adjutant) now (January 13, 1916) Assistant Adjutant and Quartermaster-General, with rank of Lieutenant-Colonel—D.S.O.

Staff Quartermaster-Sergeant C. Dyer (Divisional Train)— Médaille Militaire.

150 East Lancashire Territorial Division

FIELD AMBULANCE (ROYAL ARMY MEDICAL CORPS)
NO. 18 FIELD AMBULANCE (SPECIAL RESERVE)

Lieutenant-Colonel W. THORBURN, F.R.C.S., A.M.S., formerly on the staff of 2nd Western General Military Hospital (Manchester), now consulting surgeon to Mediterranean Expeditionary Force—C.B.

Captain W. R. DOUGLAS, M.B.—Military Cross.

Lieutenant K. W. JONES, M.D., 18th Field Ambulance—D.S.O.

Quartermaster and Hon. Lieutenant H. DUGDALE, 18th Field Ambulance—Military Cross.

Captain F. S. BEDALE, M.B.—Military Cross.

Corporal T. FEARING—D.C.M.

Private A. POOLE—D.C.M.

Quartermaster-Sergeant G. CARROLL—Médaille Militaire.

Mentioned in Dispatches—Private G. A. WALTON; Private H. PRICE; Private J. MORRIS.

EAST LANCASHIRE TERRITORIALS
Roll of Honour

> " But no ! the brave
> Die never. Being deathless, they but change
> Their country's arms for more, their country's heart."

In this " Roll of Honour " the author is conscious of one serious omission. It does not contain the names of the non-commissioned ranks. This was unavoidable and is regretted. A serious attempt had been made to compile a list of the " other ranks," but it had reluctantly to be abandoned because of the many difficulties in the way to completeness. It is hoped that at a later date an opportunity may occur to make good this omission. In the case of the officers' roll one cannot claim that it has the merit of completeness.

1ST EAST LANCASHIRE BRIGADE R.F.A.

Killed in Action.—Lieut. J. Bury, 5th Lancashire Battery (Church).

EAST LANCASHIRE DIVISIONAL ENGINEERS

Killed in Action.—Capt. Oswald Armitage Carver ; Lieut. G. J. O. Bull ; Second Lieuts. K. E. D. Ainley ; R. B. Angus.

Accidentally Killed on Suez Canal.—Second Lieut. B. H. Woods.

Died of Wounds.—Lieuts. Oscar Taunton ; L. A. Mackenzie.

5TH BATTALION LANCASHIRE FUSILIERS

Killed in Action.—Capts. S. H. Milnes ; Paton (attached) ; Lieuts. F. Whitham ; A. Renshaw ; W. C. Yapp ; A. Hinckley ; H. K. Hoyle ; E. S. Frizelle.

6TH BATTALION LANCASHIRE FUSILIERS

Killed in Action.—Capt. A. L. Spafford (Adjutant); Capt. and Quartermaster W. H. Griffiths; Capt. Victor Clegg; Lieuts. T. R. Taylor; J. H. Smith; S. O'Neill.
Died of Wounds.—Lieut. N. V. Holden.
Missing, Believed Killed.—Second Lieut. E. Duckworth.

7TH BATTALION LANCASHIRE FUSILIERS

Killed in Action.—Maj. (temp. Lieut.-Col.) W. J. Law; Capts. A. C. Humphreys; R. Waterhouse; Blease (attached); Lieut. E. W. Roberts.
Died of Wounds.—Lieuts. Bennett Burleigh; W. R. Hartley.

8TH BATTALION LANCASHIRE FUSILIERS

Killed in Action.—Lieut.-Col. J. A. Fallows; Maj. E. L. Baddeley; Capts. E. S. Humphrey; A. L. Radford (attached); Lieuts. G. A. B. Lodge; J. T. Littler; J. N. C. Morris.
Wounded and Missing.—Lieut.-Col. R. D. Waterhouse.
Died of Wounds.—Capt. A. J. Goodfellow; Lieuts. A. C. Middleton; W. V. Boydell.

5TH BATTALION MANCHESTER REGIMENT

Killed in Action.—Capt. F. S. Brown; A. C. Leech; Lieut. G. S. James; Second Lieuts. A. C. Brook; T. C. Walker.
Missing, Believed Killed.—Capt. D. D. Winterbottom; Lieut. C. Ainscough; Second Lieuts. L. E. Davis; F. L. McGeorge.
Died of Wounds.—Capt. H. M. Rogers; Lieut. F. A. James.
Killed and Died of Wounds.—Other ranks—169.

6TH BATTALION MANCHESTER REGIMENT

Killed in Action.—Capts. W. N. Bazley; J. Holt; Stanley F. Jackson; H. T. Cawley; Hugh B. Pilkington; Edgar Kessler; R. G. Edgar; A. D. Hunter; Lieuts. A. C. Brooke Taylor; E. F. Thorburn; E. T. Young; T. R. Mills; R. Killick; A. J. I. Donald; R. C. Brooks; H. W. Milne.

Roll of Honour

Died of Wounds.—Hon. Col. (Brigadier-General) Noel Lee; Lieuts. R. N. Compton Smith; W. E. Reiss.

Missing.—Lieuts. S. McDougall; J. Rainbow; L. H. Barber.

Died (during Training in this Country).—Colonel Bertram C. P. Heywood, formerly Commander of the 6th Manchesters and later Colonel Commanding the Manchester Infantry Brigade. Just before his death he had been appointed to one of the special Battalions raised in Manchester.

Killed and Died of Wounds.—Other ranks—208.

7TH BATTALION MANCHESTER REGIMENT

Killed in Action.—Maj. J. H. Staveacre; Capts. T. W. Savatard; R. V. Rylands; Lieuts. W. G. Freemantle; H. D. Thewlis; A. H. Bacon; C. L. Dudley; T. F. Brown; Davidson (attached); H. M. Granger; F. Lomas.

Missing, Believed Killed.—Lieut. G. H. Ward.

Killed and Died of Wounds.—Other ranks—228.

8TH BATTALION MANCHESTER REGIMENT

Killed in Action.—Lieut.-Col. W. G. Heys; Capts. E. G. W. Oldfield; H. J. Rose; A. J. Hepburn; Lieuts. S. Heywood; S. Hall; J. W. Womersley (signalling officer); R. Marsden (scout officer); W. H. Ingram; F. Helm; W. Norris; W. J. de Vere Scott (Lieut. Scott joined the Battalion at Cairo. He was lecturer in history at the University there); E. W. Westbrook.

Died of Wounds.—Capt. Dudley Standring; Lieut. P. C. Johnson (machine-gun officer).

Wounded and Missing.—Lieut. A. Bowen.

Casualties among Rank and File.—200 killed; 522 wounded; 41 missing.

4TH BATTALION EAST LANCASHIRE REGIMENT

Killed in Action.—Capt. H. W. Whalley; Lieuts. R. L. Whalley; P. Wolf; E. Woods; Second Lieuts. C. Coles; A. W. Fyldes.

Died of Wounds.—Lieut. W. F. Sames; Second Lieuts. F. A. Heywood; R. Smith; J. Sykes; J. Wilding.

5TH BATTALION EAST LANCASHIRE REGIMENT

Killed in Action.—Capts. H. H. Bolton and Moult; Lieuts. G. E. Sprake and J. J. Barker.

Offered Himself as a Sacrifice to Save Others.—Lieut. Alfred Victor Smith.

Died of Wounds.—Lieut. J. Bolton; Second Lieut. F. Stansfield.

Reported Missing.—Capt. S. H. Walmsley; Lieut. A. E. Rodgers.

9TH BATTALION MANCHESTER REGIMENT

Killed in Action.—Capt. Frank Hamer; Lieuts. A. E. Stringer; F. Jones.

Died of Wounds.—Capt. H. Sugden; Second Lieut. A. H. Hudson.

Reported Missing, Believed Killed.—Lieut. J. M. Wade.

Died.—Maj. W. H. Archbutt; Maj. Hilton (Medical Officer); Lieut. P. A. Woodhouse; Lieut. J. M. Robson; Lieut.-Col. T. H. Cunliffe (Second Line Battalion, died during training in this country).

Killed and Died of Wounds.—Other ranks—106.

10TH BATTALION MANCHESTER REGIMENT

Killed in Action.—Capts. G. W. Owen; J. H. Clegg; Second Lieuts. R. G. L. Ascroft; T. Kirk.

Died of Wounds.—Lieuts. J. Clegg; F. N. G. Griffiths; H. K. B. Nevinson.

Missing.—Lieut. J. Stott.

Killed in Motor Accident.—Lieut. Joseph Kirk.

Killed and Died of Wounds.—Other ranks—159.

FIELD AMBULANCES (R.A.M.C.)

Died of Wounds.—Lieut.-Col. W. B. Pritchard.

APPENDIX

THE OPERATIONS IN EGYPT

FIVE dispatches from General Sir John Maxwell relating to operations on the Egyptian frontier were published on June 22, 1916. In a long list of officers and men whose conduct is officially brought to notice are the following :

19th Lancashire Battery, R.F.A. (Bolton Artillery).—This battery rendered excellent service and was well commanded by Major B. Palin Dobson, who was ably supported by Captain P. K. Clapham, his senior officer.

Royal Artillery.—Staff-Colonel (temporary Brigadier-General) A. D'A. King, Commander of the East Lancashire Divisional Artillery (T.F.).

1st East Lancashire Brigade (The Blackburn Artillery).—Major R. B. Bickerdike, Commander of the 4th Lancashire Battery.

1st East Lancashire Field Company Royal Engineers (Old Trafford, Manchester).—Major J. H. Mousley ; 2nd East Lancashire Field Company, Major L. F. Wells.

7th Battalion Manchester Regiment.—Captain and Brevet Major (temporary Lieutenant-Colonel) J. N. Brown, Embarkation Staff Officer at Alexandria.

Manchester Regiment (Territorial Force).—No. 994 Sergeant J. Wood.

1st East Lancashire Divisional Field Ambulance (Manchester).—Captain W. R. Douglas, M.B.

www.ingramcontent.com/pod-product-compliance
Lightning Source LLC
Chambersburg PA
CBHW040301170426
43193CB00021B/2975